Best Easy Day Hikes Series

Best Easy Day Hikes Carlsbad Caverns and Guadalupe Mountains National Parks

Stewart M. Green

FALCONGUIDES

GUILFORD, CONNECTICUT

FALCONGUIDES®

An imprint of The Rowman & Littlefield Publishing Group, Inc.

4501 Forbes Blvd., Ste. 200, Lanham, MD 20706

Falcon and FalconGuides are registered trademarks and Make Adventure Your Story is a trademark of The Rowman & Littlefield Publishing Group, Inc.

Distributed by NATIONAL BOOK NETWORK

British Library Cataloguing in Publication Information available

Library of Congress Cataloging-in-Publication Data
Names: Green, Stewart M., author.
Title: Best Easy Day Hikes Carlsbad Caverns and Guadalupe Mountains National Parks / Stewart M. Green.
Description: Guilford, Connecticut : FalconGuides, 2018.
Identifiers: LCCN 2017051073 (print) | LCCN 2017052460 (ebook) | ISBN 9781493030170 (e-book) | ISBN 9781493030163 (pbk.) | ISBN 9781493030170 (ebook)
Subjects: LCSH: Day hiking—New Mexico—Carlsbad Caverns National Park—Guidebooks. | Day hiking—Texas—Guadalupe Mountains National Park—Guidebooks. | Trails—New Mexico—Carlsbad Caverns National Park—Guidebooks. | Trails—Texas—Guadalupe Mountains National Park—Guidebooks | Carlsbad Caverns National Park (N.M.)—Guidebooks. | Guadalupe Mountains National Park (Tex.)—Guidebooks.
Classification: LCC GV199.42.N62 (ebook) | LCC GV199.42.N62 G834 2018 (print) | DDC 796.510978—dc23
LC record available at https://lccn.loc.gov/2017051073

∞™ The paper used in this publication meets the minimum requirements of American National Standard for Information Sciences—Permanence of Paper for Printed Library Materials, ANSI/NISO Z39.48-1992.

Printed in the United States of America

The author and Rowman & Littlefield assume no liability for accidents happening to, or injuries sustained by, readers who engage in the activities described in this book.

Contents

Introduction 1
   Weather 1
   Types of Hikes 3
   Trail Maps 3
   Leave No Trace 4
   Be Prepared 5
   Ranking the Hikes 8
   Notes on Maps 9

Trail Finder 10

Guadalupe Mountains National Park 13
   Finding the Park and Trailheads 14
   Seasons and Weather 15
   Camping 16
   Guadalupe Ridge Trail 17

**Pine Springs and Headquarters–Visitor
Center Trailheads** 18
   1. The Pinery Trail 19
   2. Devil's Hall Trail 23
   3. Guadalupe Peak Trail 28

Frijole Ranch Trailhead 33
   4. Manzanita Spring Trail 34
   5. Smith Spring Trail 39
   6. Frijole-Foothills Trail Loop 44

McKittrick Canyon Trailhead 49
   7. McKittrick Canyon Nature Trail 50
   8. McKittrick Canyon Trail 54
   9. Permian Reef Trail 61

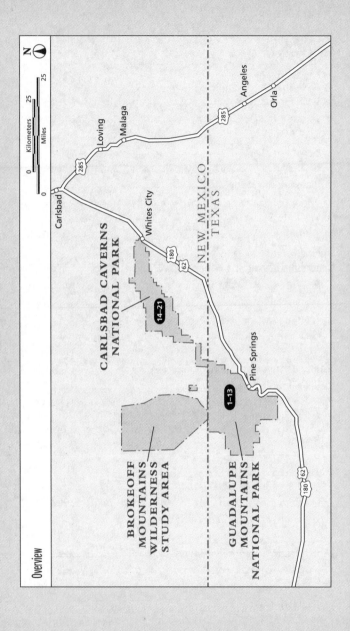

Overview

Salt Basin Dunes Trailhead 68
  10. Salt Basin Dunes Trail 69

Dog Canyon Trailhead 74
  11. Indian Meadow Nature Trail 75
  12. Bush Mountain Trail to Marcus Overlook 79
  13. Tejas Trail to Lost Peak 84

Carlsbad Caverns National Park 91
      Hiking in Carlsbad Caverns National Park 91
      Finding the Park and Trailheads 92
      Best Seasons 93
      Camping 94
  14. Chihuahuan Desert Nature Trail 95
  15. Walnut Canyon Vista Trail 100
  16. Old Guano Road Trail 103
  17. Juniper Ridge Trail 108
  18. Rattlesnake Canyon Trail 112

Cave Trails 117
  19. Natural Entrance Trail 118
  20. Big Room Trail 124
  21. King's Palace Trail 131

Appendix: Trail Contact Information 137
About the Author 138

Map Legend

═══⟨62⟩═══	US Highway
═══⟨7⟩═══	State Highway
═══⟨418⟩═══	Local/Forest Roads
════	Unimproved Road
-------	Trail
━━━━━━━	Featured Route
[_ _]	National Forest/National Park
⏝	Bridge
▲	Campground
♿	Handicap-accessible
❓	Information
🅿	Parking
⏜	Pass
▲	Peak
🏕	Picnic Area
■	Point of Interest/Other Trailhead
▲	Primitive Campground
⌀	Spring
❶	Trailhead
⬕	Viewpoint
≋	Waterfall

Introduction

Guadalupe Mountains and Carlsbad Caverns National Parks, lying along the Texas and New Mexico border, are two parklands that offer different hiking experiences. Guadalupe Mountains is a rugged area of high mountains and deep canyons that are traversed by over 80 miles of trails. The park offers trails up two iconic Texas landmarks—Guadalupe Peak, the state's highest point, and McKittrick Canyon, sometimes called the most beautiful spot in Texas. Carlsbad Caverns offers spectacular hikes into the famous cave as well as trails that explore surrounding canyons. *Best Easy Day Hikes Carlsbad Caverns and Guadalupe Mountains National Parks* describes twenty-one of the best and most accessible trails for the casual hiker in search of adventure.

If you are on a tight schedule or want to do a short, excellent hike in a scenic park area, this book allows you to quickly select a hike suited to your abilities and time constraints. Most of the hikes are between 1 and 5 miles long. Also included are easy walks for families and barrier-free trails that are wheelchair accessible. All of the trailheads are easily accessible by car and have parking lots.

The hikes are rated by difficulty from easiest to most challenging. Check the listing to help you decide which hike is best for you and your party.

Weather

All the hikes in Guadalupe Mountains and Carlsbad Caverns National Parks lie in the northern Chihuahuan Desert, one of North America's five great deserts. This high desert is wetter and cooler than other deserts like southern Arizona's

Sonoran Desert. The best hiking months are September and October and April and May, although summers are generally pleasant at Guadalupe Mountains National Park with its high elevations.

Temperature and precipitation at Guadalupe Mountains National Park greatly varies depending on elevation, which ranges from 3,000 feet at Salt Basin to 8,751 feet atop Guadalupe Peak, the highest point in Texas. Hiking is good year-round, with cool temperatures between November and March and warm temperatures from April through October. Summer temperatures are hot in the sun, with daily highs averaging 88°F in June and July at Pine Springs. The shoulder months of April and October are perfect for hiking with highs averaging 73°F. Most of the park's 17.4 inches of annual precipitation falls during the summer monsoon season from June through September. Watch for heavy thunderstorms accompanied by lightning during the summer. Late fall and winter offers good hiking weather but expect high winds over 70 mph, especially at high elevations. Snow also falls in the colder months, but usually melts except on north-facing slopes. It's best to dress in layers when hiking, as well as wear a hat and sunscreen, and carry plenty of water and sports drinks.

Carlsbad Caverns National Park, with elevations ranging between 3,600 feet and 6,500 feet, has a semiarid climate with hot summers and mild, dry winters. The best hiking months are between October and April. Summer high temperatures are in the 90s and low 100s, with an average high in June and July of 90°F. Most of the park's annual 14.9 inches of precipitation falls in heavy thunderstorms between July and September during the monsoon season. Plan summer hikes for the early morning or evening when temperatures are much cooler than the middle of the day. Almost no shade is found on any of the surface hikes, so bring plenty of water and sports drinks, and wear sunscreen and a hat for protection.

The cavern hikes are cooler than surface trails, with a year-round temperature of 56°F on the described trails and humidity varying between 87 percent in winter to 95 percent in summer. Most hikers are comfortable wearing a light sweater or sweatshirt.

Types of Hikes

Loop: A loop hike starts and ends at the same trailhead via different routes, although part of the hike may retrace the same route for a short distance.

Out and back: An out-and-back hike reaches a specific destination and returns via the same route. Distances given in the text are specified as one-way (just the out portion) or round-trip (out and back).

Lollipop: A loop hike that follows the same route out and back at its start to a loop trail, forming a shape like a kid's lollipop.

Trail Maps

Maps of all hiking trails are included in this book. It is recommended you supplement these with more detailed maps. USGS topographic maps and National Geographic Trails Illustrated maps are listed for each hike, and both are good options. Hiking maps for popular trails may be available at visitor centers. GPS coordinates are listed for parking areas, trailheads, major trail junctions, points of interest, and turn-around points for all the hikes.

Leave No Trace

The Guadalupe Mountains, including the Carlsbad Caverns area, lie in the Chihuahuan Desert ecosystem, an area characterized by hot temperatures and plants like the creosote bush, agave, and various cacti species. Desert ecosystems and environments are extremely fragile and sensitive to human use. The marks of humans linger for a long time on this arid landscape, including old mines, social trails, and damage from off-road vehicles and motorcycles.

National parks are natural areas mostly unspoiled by human impacts. It's important to practice a Leave No Trace ethic to protect the area's natural resources and trails from overuse, to maintain a positive experience for other visitors, to preserve natural areas and wilderness, and to protect wildlife.

Leave No Trace is about responsible outdoor ethics, including staying on the trail, not cutting switchbacks, packing out litter, proper disposal of human waste, and leaving the environment as pristine as possible. It's our responsibility to pay attention to our impact so that we can ensure that these national parks and their trails will remain as wild refuges from the urban environment.

Follow these Leave No Trace guidelines to lessen your impact:

- Always stay on the trail. Cutting switchbacks or traveling cross-country causes erosion and destroys plants. Always follow the established route whenever possible. Steep slopes are susceptible to erosion caused by off-trail hiking.
- Pack it in—pack it out. Everything you carry and use, including food wrappers, orange peels, cigarette butts,

plastic bottles, and energy bar wrappers, needs to come out with you. Carry a plastic bag for picking up trash along the trail.

- Respect public and private property, livestock fences, and mining claims. Federal laws protect all archaeological and historic antiquities, including Native American artifacts, projectile points, ruins, petroglyphs and pictographs, petrified wood, and historic sites. Don't carve your name in a rock surface or on a tree.

- Properly dispose human waste by bringing at least two WAG bags per hiker for backcountry use. A WAG bag is a poop disposal system with a waste collection bag and a disposal bag. Carry used WAG bags out for sanitary disposal. In an emergency, dig a six-inch-deep hole that's at least 300 feet from water sources, dry washes, campsites, and trails. Do not burn or bury toilet paper. Instead, pack it out in a plastic baggie. The best thing to do is to use the public restrooms found at many trailheads.

- Take only photographs and memories. Avoid leaving evidence of our passage across this delicate desert and mountain environment. With care and sensitivity, we can all do our part to keep the national parks beautiful, clean, and pristine. Leave natural features such as flowers or rocks where you found them. Enjoy their beauty, but leave them for the next hiker. Besides being unlawful, if everyone took one item, it wouldn't be long before nothing was left for others to enjoy.

Be Prepared

Hiking, although immensely rewarding, also comes with hazards and inherent risks, especially for those who are unprepared. Respect the mountain and desert environments. Be prepared and you'll help ensure your safety.

You must assume responsibility for your own actions and for your safety. Be aware of your surroundings and of potential dangers, including drop-offs, cliffs, loose rock, the weather, and the physical condition of both your party and yourself. Never be afraid to turn around if conditions aren't right. Pay attention to those instincts and gut feelings—they could keep you alive. Hike smart.

Here are suggestions to be prepared for emergency situations on your hike:

- Bring extra clothes and a raincoat, especially in the mountains. The weather can change in an instant. Heavy thunderstorms regularly occur on summer afternoons, and cold, wet clothing can lead to hypothermia or a cooling of the body's core.

- Summer brings thunderstorms and lightning strikes to the parks. Pay attention to the weather, and get off high places, ridges, and open areas before a storm arrives. If you can hear thunder, it's probably not safe to be outdoors.

- The sun is bright in the desert. Summer temperatures are usually hot. Wear a hat and use sunscreen to avoid sunburn and wear loose-fitting clothing to stay cool.

- Carry plenty of water and sports drinks to replace electrolytes lost through sweating. Bring at least a gallon of liquid per person for a day-long summer hike or two quarts for a half-day hike. Don't drink any water from streams or springs unless you first treat and purify it. Heat exhaustion and heatstroke may occur during strenuous exercise in hot summer temperatures. Avoid these life-threatening conditions by drinking regularly, eat high carbohydrate foods for energy, avoid high temperatures and humidity, wear light-colored clothes and a hat, and don't drink alcohol or caffeine.

- If you're coming from a lower elevation, watch for symptoms of altitude sickness, including headache, nausea, and loss of appetite, on the high mountains. The best cure is to lose elevation.

- Allow enough time for your hike. If you start in late afternoon, bring a headlamp or flashlight so that you can see the trail in the dark.

- Bring plenty of high-energy snacks for the trail and treats for the youngsters.

- Wear comfortable hiking shoes and good socks. To avoid blisters, break in your shoes before wearing them in the backcountry. Avoid wearing sandals—the trails are rough and stony.

- Enjoy the wildlife you see along the trail, but keep your distance and treat the animals with respect. Some animals bite and spread diseases like rabies. Watchful mothers, including deer and bears, are protective of their babies. Don't feed wildlife to avoid disrupting their natural eating habits.

- Five species of rattlesnakes frequent park trails, so watch where you place your hands and feet. Stay on trails where rattlers are easily seen. Move around any rattlesnake and continue hiking. It's illegal to kill or harm rattlesnakes in the parks.

- Mountain lions live in the national parks and may be seen at Guadalupe Mountains, especially the Dog Canyon area. Lions are rarely spotted but may be encountered. When hiking in mountain lion country, travel in groups and keep children close and within sight at all times. Don't let them run ahead. If you encounter a lion, move back slowly, don't run, raise your arms to appear bigger, pick up children, avoid eye contact, and throw stones and branches if it acts aggressively.

- Carry a day pack to tote all your trail needs, including rain gear, food, water, a first-aid kit, a flashlight or head-lamp, matches, and extra clothes. A whistle, GPS unit or compass, topographic map, binoculars, camera, pocket-knife, and FalconGuide identification books for plants and animals are all handy additions. And don't forget your copy of *Best Easy Day Hikes Carlsbad Caverns and Guadalupe Mountains National Parks*!

Ranking the Hikes

The hikes in this book range from easy to more challenging, depending on the length of the hike as well as the elevation gain. Remember, most challenging hikes can be made easier by simply turning around early in the hike. Here's a list of all the hikes from easiest to most challenging:

20. The Big Room Trail
21. King's Palace Trail (ranger-led only)
15. Walnut Canyon Vista Trail
 4. Manzanita Spring Trail
 1. The Pinery Trail
19. Natural Entrance Trail
14. Chihuahuan Desert Nature Trail
11. Indian Meadow Nature Trail
 7. McKittrick Canyon Nature Trail
10. Salt Basin Dunes Trail
16. Old Guano Road Trail

17. Juniper Ridge Trail

 6. Frijole-Foothills Trails Loop

 5. Smith Spring Trail

18. Rattlesnake Canyon Trail

 2. Devil's Hall Trail

 8. McKittrick Canyon Trail

12. Bush Mountain Trail to Marcus Overlook

13. Tejas Trail to Lost Peak

 9. Permian Reef Trail

 3. Guadalupe Peak Trail

Notes on Maps

Topographic maps are essential companions to the activities in this guide. Falcon has partnered with National Geographic to provide the best mapping resources. Each activity is accompanied by a detailed map and the name of the National Geographic TOPO! map (USGS), which can be downloaded for free from natgeomaps.com.

If the activity takes place on a National Geographic Trails Illustrated map, it will be noted. Continually setting the standard for accuracy, each Trails Illustrated topographic map is crafted in conjunction with local land managers and undergoes rigorous review and enhancement before being printed on waterproof, tear-resistant material. Trails Illustrated maps and information about their digital versions, which can be used on mobile GPS applications, can be found at natgeomaps.com.

Trail Finder

Best Hikes for Families
1. The Pinery Trail
5. Smith Spring Trail
7. McKittrick Canyon Nature Trail
11. Indian Meadow Nature Trail
14. Chihuahuan Desert Nature Trail

Best Hikes for Wheelchairs
4. Manzanita Spring Trail
14. Chihuahuan Desert Nature Trail
20. The Big Room Trail

Best Hikes for Scenery
3. Guadalupe Peak Trail
8. McKittrick Canyon Trail
9. Permian Reef Trail
18. Rattlesnake Canyon Trail
20. The Big Room Trail

Best Hikes for Views
3. Guadalupe Peak Trail
8. McKittrick Canyon Trail
12. Bush Mountain to Marcus Overlook
13. Tejas Trail to Lost Peak
18. Rattlesnake Canyon Trail

Best Hikes for Geology
2. Devil's Hall Trail
9. Permian Reef Trail
10. Salt Basin Dunes Trail
19. Natural Entrance Trail
20. The Big Room Trail

Best Hikes for Photography

3.   Guadalupe Peak Trail
2.   Devil's Hall Trail
8.   McKittrick Canyon Trail
10.   Salt Basin Dunes Trail
20.   The Big Room Trail

Best Hikes for Backpacking

3.   Guadalupe Peak Trail
9.   Permian Reef Trail
13.   Tejas Trail to Lost Peak to either McKittrick Canyon Trail or Pine Springs Trailhead
18.   Rattlesnake Canyon Trail

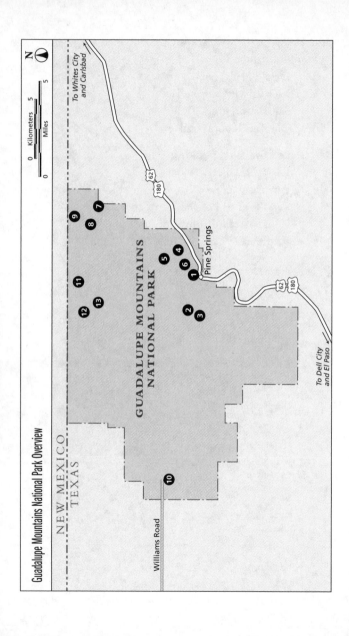

Guadalupe Mountains National Park Overview

N

0 Kilometers 5
0 Miles 5

To Whites City
and Carlsbad

62
180

Pine Springs

62
180

To Dell City
and El Paso

GUADALUPE MOUNTAINS
NATIONAL PARK

NEW MEXICO
TEXAS

Williams Road

Guadalupe Mountains National Park

Guadalupe Mountains National Park spreads across 86,367 acres of dramatic mountains, deep canyons, scrubby valleys, and shady glades filled with birdsong in west Texas. The park, bounded by US 62/180 on the south and the New Mexico border on the north, is an enclave of superlatives with the four highest peaks in Texas, one of the world's largest fossil reefs, an imposing limestone wall called El Capitan, and McKittrick Canyon, a place dubbed the most beautiful spot in Texas. Most of the national park is a designated wilderness area that's explored by lacing up your boots and walking on over 80 miles of trails, making it a paradise for hikers and backpackers.

The southern part of the national park at Pine Springs, lying 110 miles east of El Paso and 55 miles southwest of Carlsbad, New Mexico, is remote and uncluttered compared to other national parklands. Visitation over the twenty years between 1996 and 2017 placed Guadalupe Mountains National Park as the forty-seventh most popular park out of the nation's fifty-nine national parks, with a mere 181,839 visitors in 2016, compared to 13.2 million at Great Smoky Mountains and 5.9 million at Grand Canyon. The park was established on September 30, 1972.

The park's relative remoteness and low visitation keep it wild and off-the-beaten track. You're not going to see buses filled with photo-snapping tourists at the park's seven parking lots, and there aren't any motels, restaurants, gift shops, or RV parks nearby. Instead you'll find two small campgrounds with basic tent and RV/trailer spaces, trails where you'll rarely see other hikers, and lots of solitude and wildlife.

The twenty named trails in Guadalupe Mountains National Park offer plenty of adventures from easy hikes on nature trails to full-day treks that climb to pine forests and airy mountain tops. It's easy to loop several trails together to make multiday backpacking trips across the park. This book details thirteen day hikes, including easy kid-friendly trails, a handicap-accessible trail to Manzanita Spring, and the two most popular hikes in the park at McKittrick Canyon and up to the rocky summit of 8,751-foot Guadalupe Peak, the highest point in Texas. The hikes begin from five trailheads in the park—Pine Springs, Frijole Ranch, McKittrick Canyon, Dog Canyon, and Salt Basin Dunes.

Finding the Park and Trailheads

The main visitor center at Guadalupe Mountains National Park is at the Pine Springs area on the north side of US 62/180 about 55 miles southwest of Carlsbad, New Mexico, and 110 miles east of El Paso, which is served by major airlines. Your first stop should be the visitor center to acquaint yourself with the park, pick up maps, get ranger advice, and explore the park's plants, animals, and geology in a small museum. The Pine Springs Trailhead, with park information, restrooms, and water, and Pine Springs Campground are northwest of the visitor center. Four trails begin here—El Capitan, Guadalupe Peak, Devil's Hall, and Tejas trails.

McKittrick Canyon and its trailhead is a day-use only area 7 miles east of the visitor center off US 62/180. The McKittrick Road runs 4.5 miles north to a small visitor center, with park information, restrooms, and water. The McKittrick Canyon area is open from 8 a.m. to 6 p.m. from early to mid-March through early November, and from 8 a.m. to 4:30 p.m. from November to March. Gate hours change with daylight savings time and standard time. Allow enough time to hike the three described trails so you can leave before the posted closing time. The entrance gate on US 62/180 is locked every evening.

Frijole Ranch Trailhead is 1.4 miles east of the visitor center off US 62/180. The Frijole Ranch History Museum, a nineteenth-century ranch, is an educational stop to discover the human history of the Guadalupe Mountains. It's usually open daily from 8 a.m. to 4:30 p.m. Three hikes begin at the trailhead, which has water, restrooms, and picnic tables.

Dog Canyon Trailhead, located on the northern edge of the park, is over 100 miles from the Pine Springs area. Drive to Carlsbad, New Mexico, and then go north on US 285 for 12 miles. Turn west on New Mexico 137 and drive 58 miles to Dog Canyon Visitor Center, campground, and trailhead.

The Salt Basin Dunes Trailhead, 47 miles from the visitor center, lies in the Salt Basin area on the western side of the park. Drive west on US 62/180 for 23 miles to Salt Flat. Turn north on FM Road 1576 and drive 17 miles to William's Road. Turn east and drive 7.5 miles to the trailhead. The last dirt road section may be impassable after rain.

Seasons and Weather

Good hiking is found year-round at Guadalupe Mountains National Park with its wide range of elevations, but the best times are April to May and September to mid-November. The autumn is especially beautiful with calm days and color-ful fall foliage in the canyons.

The Guadalupe Mountains are characterized by hot summers, mild autumns, cool to cold winters, and cool springs. Daily highs average in the mid-80s in the summer months, and in the 70s during the shoulder months. Winter temperatures are in the low 50s in December through February. The record high temperature is 105°F, while the record low is 0°F.

Snow, freezing rain, and fog occur during the winter. The mountains, especially the high ridges and summits, are often windy in winter and spring. The national park is one of the windiest places in the United States. Monsoon moisture pushes up from Mexico in July and August, creating extreme thunderstorms accompanied by lightning in the afternoon and evening.

Camping

Guadalupe Mountains National Park offers two campgrounds. The Pine Springs Campground near the visitor center and Pine Springs Trailhead has twenty tent sites and twenty RV sites, which accommodate vehicles up to 50 feet. It has accessible sites, a stock corral, restrooms, and water. The Dog Canyon Campground on the far north side of the park has nine tent sites and four RV sites. It has an accessible site, restrooms, water, and a nearby stock corral.

There are no reservations for any campsites. All sites are on a first-come first-served basis. Fires and charcoal fires are not allowed at the campgrounds or in the park at any time because of high fire danger. All cooking must be done on contained propane or gas stoves and grills. Generators are permitted between 8 a.m. and 8 p.m. at designated areas only. Two group campsites for ten to twenty people are available at Pine Springs and can be reserved up to sixty days in advance by calling (915) 828-3251.

Guadalupe Ridge Trail

As of 2018, the Guadalupe Ridge Trail is mapped and being developed for hiking adventures. This hundred-mile trail runs from Guadalupe Peak in Guadalupe Mountains National Park to the east side of Carlsbad Caverns National Park at Whites City in New Mexico. The trail crosses two national parks, the Guadalupe District of the Lincoln National Forest, and parcels of land managed by the Bureau of Land Management. Whether you hike short sections of the trail over a series of separate one- or two-day trips or walk the entire trail in a week-long trek, the Guadalupe Ridge Trail offers an extreme hiking challenge, outstanding opportunities for solitude, and spectacular views from the crest of the Guadalupe Mountains that few visitors experience. Some trail sections require route-finding skills and water caches to navigate the dry mountains. Check with Guadalupe Mountains and Carlsbad Caverns National Parks for trail information and maps.

Pine Springs and Headquarters–Visitor Center Trailheads

1 The Pinery Trail

An easy, self-guided, interpretive trail between the Pine Springs Visitor Center and The Pinery, an old stagecoach-changing station.

Distance: 0.9 mile or 0.7 mile if you hike only the paved trail out and back

Hiking time: 1 hour

Type of hike: Out-and-back lollipop trail; paved trail surface

Difficulty: Easy; ADA handicap- and wheelchair-accessible

Elevation gain: 100 feet

Best seasons: Year-round. Summer days can be hot, with no shade on the trail.

Restrictions: Open year-round with no restrictions. Dogs allowed on a leash. Pick up all dog waste.

Maps: Guadalupe Peak USGS Quad; 203 National Geographic/ Trails Illustrated Guadalupe Mountains National Park Trail Map; park map

Trail contact: Guadalupe Mountains National Park (see appendix)

Finding the trailhead: Turn north from US 62/180 at a sign that reads "Guadalupe Mtns National Park Headquarters Visitors Ctr." Drive north for 0.15 mile to a large parking lot and the Headquarters-Visitor Center Trailhead. Walk on a paved trail for 200 feet to the west side of the visitor center and the start of the hike. Trailhead GPS: N31 53.39'/ W104 49.19'

The Hike

The 0.9-mile Pinery Trail is a fun out-and-back hike that loops around the ruins of The Pinery Station, a stagecoach stop on the Butterfield Overland Mail route in the 1850s. The easy hike follows a paved, ADA-accessible trail from Pine Springs Visitor Center along the south bank of a wide, dry wash. The trail is great for families and senior citizens, with good views of the surrounding mountains and signs that interpret the flora and fauna of the Chihuahuan Desert. No shade is found along the trail, so hike in morning or evening on hot days, wear a hat, and bring water. Pets are allowed on a leash.

Begin the hike on the west side of the Pine Springs Visitor Center just north of US 62/180. A large parking lot is 200 feet to the southwest of the center. Go right on the paved trail and follow it along the southern edge of a wide, sandy wash that drains southeast from Pine Springs Canyon in the Guadalupe Mountains to the north. The trail passes signs that explain the area's plants, including cacti, shrubs, and trees.

The trail reaches a T-junction after 0.35 mile. Go left on the paved trail. A right turn leads 180 feet to a large parking area alongside US 62/180. Walk 185 feet to the end of the paved trail and the first ruins, a section of a tall wall that once surrounded the Butterfield Stage Station. This is the turn-around spot for wheelchairs and the end of the accessible trail. The round-trip hike from the visitor center to this point and back is 0.75 mile. The next section follows a rougher 0.15-mile loop trail, which returns to the T-junction.

The Pinery, or Pinery Station, was a relay station on the Butterfield Overland Mail stagecoach route. The station, built in 1858 and abandoned the next year, began as a military outpost in 1849. It had a three-room station house, blacksmith shop, wagon repair shop, and large pine-log corral surrounded by 11-foot-high stone walls for protection from raiding Mescalero Apaches. Coaches stopped for teams of fresh horses and hot meals for passengers and crews. Water from Pine Spring flowed down a ditch to a tank at

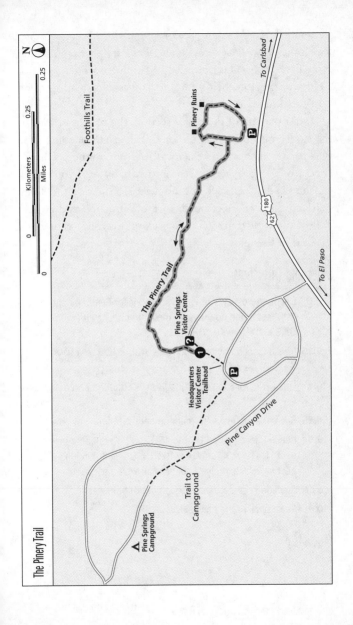

The Pinery Trail

Pine Springs Campground

Trail to Campground

Pine Canyon Drive

Headquarters Visitor Center Trailhead

Pine Springs Visitor Center

The Pinery Trail

Pinery Ruins

Foothills Trail

To El Paso

To Carlsbad

62 180

Kilometers
0   0.25
Miles
0   0.25

N

the station. Traffic along the route included stagecoaches four times a week, express mail riders, freight wagons, and mule pack trains. The Butterfield Mail line operated here for 11 months, before being rerouted on a safer road through Fort Stockton and Fort Davis.

From the end of the paved section, the trail heads east to the stone ruins of a small building. Turn right or south here on a narrow path and hike across flat terrain to the northwest corner of a large parking area on the highway. If you have a car shuttle, they can pick you up here. Go right on the paved trail and walk 180 feet north to the T-junction and go left. Follow the wide trail 0.35 mile back to the visitor center and the end of the hike.

Miles and Directions

0.0 Begin on west side of Pine Springs Visitor Center, about 200 feet to the northeast of the main parking lot (GPS: N31 53.39' / W104 49.19').

0.35 Reach junction of loop trail (GPS: N31 53.39' / W104 49.19'). Go left.

0.4 First set of ruins on right. This is the end of the paved trail. Go right.

0.45 Second set of ruins. Go right on narrow trail.

0.5 Reach parking lot on US 62/180 and paved Pinery Trail (GPS: N31 53.35' / W104 49.01'). Go right or north. Alternatively, end hike at parking lot with a car shuttle.

0.55 Junction at start of loop. Go left to visitor center.

0.9 Arrive back at the trailhead.

2 Devil's Hall Trail

An excellent out-and-back trail along a dry wash to Devil's Hall, a narrow 200-foot-long canyon lined with limestone cliffs.

Distance: 4.2 miles out and back

Hiking time: 3–5 hours

Difficulty: Moderate

Elevation gain: 548 feet

Type of hike: Out-and-back

Best seasons: Year-round. Summer days can be hot. Watch for flash floods after thunderstorms.

Restrictions: Open year-round with no restrictions. Dogs not allowed. Horses follow the first section to the alternative Guadalupe Peak Trail.

Maps: Guadalupe Peak USGS Quad; 203 National Geographic/Trails Illustrated Guadalupe Mountains National Park Trail Map; park map

Trail contact: Guadalupe Mountains National Park (see appendix)

Finding the trailhead: From US 62/180, turn north and drive 0.6 mile, passing the turn to Pine Springs Visitor Center and the park campground, to a parking lot at the road's end. Pine Springs Trailhead is at the northwest corner of the lot. Restrooms and water are at the lot. Trailhead GPS: N31 53.47' / W104 49.41'

The Hike

Devil's Hall Trail, one of the best hikes in Guadalupe Mountains National Park, follows the floor of Pine Spring Canyon to Devil's Hall, a narrow gorge walled by limestone cliffs. The 4.2-mile round-trip hike gains 548 feet and takes about three hours to hike. The first half of the trail is easy, while the second half threads up a dry streambed, scrambling over boulders and following occasional cairns that mark the route. Do not make extra cairns along the trail. Trees line parts of the trail, providing welcome shade on warm days. Big-tooth maples, especially in the upper canyon, tint the rough land with brilliant red, orange, yellow colors in October and November.

The trail, crossing open and wooded terrain, is hot in summer. Bring plenty of water and sports drinks, a hat, and sunscreen. The second half of the hike up the streambed is rough with loose rocks and boulders. Watch for rattlesnakes along the trail in the warmer months. Heavy thunderstorms fall in the Guadalupe Mountains on summer afternoons, particularly in July and August. The streambed can flood after rain, so monitor the weather and climb to higher ground for safety.

Start the hike at the Pine Springs Trailhead at the northwest corner of a parking lot at the end of the road past the visitor center and campground. A kiosk at the trailhead has a hiker register, park map, and information. Restrooms and water are at the southwest corner of the parking lot.

Hike for 110 feet to a junction with Tejas Trail, keep left and continue to a three-way trail junction at 0.1 mile with El Capitan Trail on the left, Guadalupe Peak Trail going straight, and the Devil's Hall Trail on the right. Go right on the marked trail. The Devil's Hall Trail is the alternative Guadalupe Peak Trail for horses for its first mile, which lets equestrians avoid a steep section of switchbacks on the regular Guadalupe Peak Trail.

The first mile heads northwest along slopes south of Pine Spring Creek's dry wash. This section, used by horses, is wide and easy to follow. Occasional trees shade the trail but it crosses open country so it's usually hot in summer. The area burned in 1993 but has since recovered. At one mile, keep straight at a junction with the Guadalupe Peak Stock Trail.

The trail heads up the canyon and 0.15 mile from the junction, it bends right and descends into the stony wash below. The second half of the trail follows the dry wash northeast, scrambling around boulders. The hiking is rough and rocky, with uneven terrain. Sometimes the trail seems to disappear among the rounded boulders. Stay in the wash and follow the easiest path and you won't get lost. Watch for cairns or small stacks of rocks that occasionally mark the trail. The cairns are placed by park rangers at strategic locations along the trail. Do not build extra cairns along the trail or in the wash. Building unnecessary cairns can lead to hikers taking wrong turns as well as damage delicate ecosystems.

After 1.6 miles the canyon narrows and the trail passes through cliffs called Devil's Gate and climbs stair-stepped ledges sometimes called the Hiker's Staircase. Continue up the wash to Devil's Hall, a 15-foot-wide and 200-foot-long canyon walled by vertical limestone cliffs, and the end of the hike at 2.1 miles. This is a great spot to relax in the canyon's shade and eat a picnic lunch. The canyon was carved by flash floods tumbling boulders through a break in a thick band of limestone.

Devil's Hall Trail, besides being a geologic showcase, also offers diverse vegetation along the riparian zone in the narrow upper canyon. Numerous trees, including bigtooth maple, velvet ash, Texas madrone, and ponderosa pine, provide welcome shade and autumn colors that rival nearby McKittrick Canyon.

After resting, pack up and return down the canyon and trail to the Pine Springs Trailhead for a 4.2-mile hike.

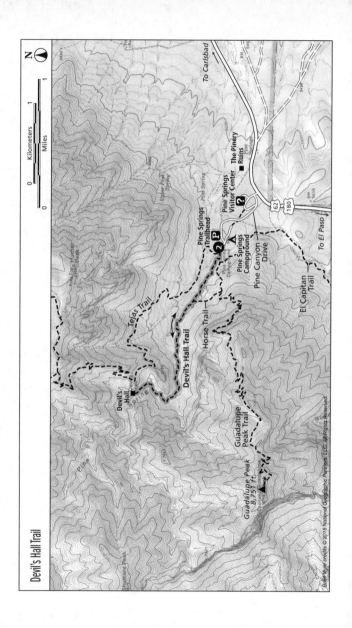

Devil's Hall Trail

Miles and Directions

0.0 Pine Springs Trailhead at northwest corner of large parking lot (GPS: N31 53.47' / W104 49.41').

125 ft Junction with Tejas Trail and Guadalupe Peak Trail. Go left on Guadalupe Peak Trail.

450 ft Three-way junction with El Capitan Trail (left), Guadalupe Peak Trail (straight), and Devil's Hall Trail (right) (GPS: N31 53.47' / W104 49.46'). Go right.

0.3 Reach south side of dry wash.

1.0 Junction with Guadalupe Peak Horse Trail (GPS: N31 54.05' / W104 50.28'). Go straight.

1.15 Trail reaches dry creek bed (GPS: N31 54 05' / W104 50 38'). Follow it northwest.

2.1 Reach Devil's Hall (GPS: N31 54.23' / W104 50.51').

4.2 Arrive back at the trailhead.

3 Guadalupe Peak Trail

This popular hike, one of the most difficult in this book, climbs a good trail to the summit of 8,751-foot Guadalupe Peak, the highest point in Texas.

Distance: 8.5 miles round-trip
Hiking time: 6–8 hours
Type of hike: Out-and-back trail
Difficulty: Strenuous
Elevation gain: 2,906 feet
Best seasons: Year-round. Best months are Oct to May. Summer is hot. Trail is often windy.
Restrictions: Open year-round with no restrictions. Dogs not allowed. Horses are allowed to within 100 feet of the summit.

Riders take an alternative trail at the start to avoid a steep 0.7-mile section.
Maps: Guadalupe Peak USGS Quad; 203 National Geographic/ Trails Illustrated Guadalupe Mountains National Park Trail Map; park map
Trail contact: Guadalupe Mountains National Park (see appendix)

Finding the trailhead: From US 62/180, turn north and drive 0.6 mile, passing the turn to Pine Springs Visitor Center and the park campground, to a parking lot at the road's end. Pine Springs Trailhead is at the northwest corner of the lot. Restrooms and water are at the lot. Trailhead GPS: N31 53.47' / W104 49.41'

The Hike

The popular 4.25-mile Guadalupe Peak Trail, climbing to the highest point in Texas, is a spectacular hike with gorgeous scenery, gentle grades, a unique summit pyramid, and expansive views. While the hike is not easy, it should be at the top of your Guadalupe Mountains National Park hike list. Most hikers with average fitness are able to hike to the 8,751-foot summit of Guadalupe Peak. As famed western writer Edward Abbey noted, "The climb by foot trail is difficult but not beyond the ability of any two-legged American, aged eight to eighty, in normal health."

The trail, gaining 2,906 feet from the Pine Springs Trailhead to the summit, is best done in the cooler months between October and May. The summer months are hot, so start early in the morning. No water is found along the trail, so carry plenty of water and sports drinks to stay hydrated. A gallon per person is not too much in summer. The trail ascends both open and wooded terrain, and most of the trail is rocky, so wear proper footwear. Watch for rattlesnakes along the trail in the warmer months. Heavy thunderstorms often occur on summer afternoons, particularly in July and August. Pay attention to the weather to avoid lightning on exposed ridges and the summit.

The Guadalupe Mountains, including Guadalupe Peak, is one of the windiest places in the United States. It is often windy during the cooler months when it's best to climb the mountain. The park brochure for climbing Guadalupe Peak warns, "Winds in excess of 80 miles per hour are not uncommon."

Begin the hike at the 5,845-foot Pine Springs Trailhead at the northwest corner of a large parking lot at the end of the road past the park visitor center and campground. A trailhead kiosk has park information, a map, and hiker register. Remember to sign out before hiking. Restrooms and water are at the southwest corner of the parking lot.

From the trailhead, hike 110 feet to a junction with Tejas Trail, keep left and continue to a three-way trail junction at 0.1 mile. Go straight on the marked Guadalupe Peak Trail. The Devil's Hall Trail and the alternative Guadalupe Peak Horse Trail go right, while the El Capitan Trail heads left.

Horses are allowed on the Guadalupe Peak Trail, but all horses must stop at a hitching post 100 feet from the summit. The elevation gain, steepness of the route, and lack of water make the ascent difficult for most horses. Equestrians use a longer horse trail on the lower part of the mountain to avoid a steep section of switchbacks. The horse trail follows Devil's Hall Trail for its first mile, and then goes left on another trail for 0.7 mile to the Guadalupe Peak Trail.

The steepest section of the trail is the first mile and a half. The trail climbs up the broad east ridge of the peak, making twenty switchbacks across rocky slopes to a shoulder on the north side of the ridge. The junction with the horse trail is halfway up the slope at 0.8 mile. After a final steep section, the trail reaches a high ridgeline and bends onto the north side of the mountain. This is a good spot to catch a rest and enjoy views into Pine Spring Canyon and across the escarpment of the Guadalupe Mountains.

The next trail section contours across the north-facing slope, passing through a shady woodland of piñon pine, white pine, and Douglas fir. The cooler slopes receive more moisture than south-facing ones, allowing the trees to flourish. The trail continues climbing and switchbacking upward and after 3 miles reaches a false summit and crosses flatter terrain.

The Guadalupe Peak Backcountry Campground, the highest campground in Texas, is reached at 3.2 miles after climbing 2,200 feet. Look for a marked trail that heads right for 0.1 mile to five designated campsites on a rounded knoll among scattered trees. The campground is renowned for great stargazing as well as fierce winds, especially in spring. Make sure to stake your tent well.

The last mile-long trail segment continues west along a ridge and then switchbacks up the south flank of the peak to the rocky 8,751-foot summit of Guadalupe Peak, the

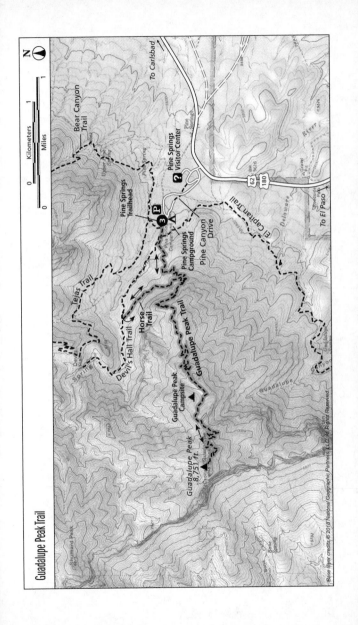

Guadalupe Peak Trail

To Carlsbad

Bear Canyon Trail

Pine Springs Trailhead

Tejas Trail

Devil's Hall Trail

Horse Trail

Pine Springs Campground

Pine Canyon Drive

Pine Springs Visitor Center

Pine Springs

Pine Springs River

62
180

To El Paso

El Capitan Trail

Guadalupe Peak Campsite

Guadalupe Peak Trail

Guadalupe Peak 8,751 ft.

Shumard Peak

N

Kilometers

Miles

0   1

Base layer credits: © 2018 National Geographic Partners, LLC. All Rights Reserved.

highest point in Texas. Expansive views spread out beyond the mountain, with 8,631-foot Bush Mountain and 8,615-foot Shumard Peak, the Lone Star State's second and third highest peaks, to the north, while the limestone block of El Capitan lies south of the summit.

Find the summit register at the base of a stainless steel pyramid and sign your name to commemorate your ascent of Guadalupe Peak. American Airlines placed the gaudy pyramid in 1958 for the hundredth anniversary of the Butterfield Overland Mail Route, a stagecoach and mail service between St. Louis and San Francisco from 1857 to 1861. The route passed south of Guadalupe Peak, stopping at The Pinery Station. The pyramid has logos for American Airlines, the Butterfield riders, and the Boy Scouts of America on its three sides.

After enjoying the view, return to the Pine Springs Trailhead by following the trail back down the mountain for an 8.2-mile, round-trip hike.

Miles and Directions

0.0 Start at the Pine Springs Trailhead at the northwest corner of a large parking lot (GPS: N31 53.47' / W104 49.41').

110 ft Junction with Tejas Trail. Go left.

0.1 Three-way junction with Devil's Hall Trail and the alternative Guadalupe Peak Horse Trail on the right and El Capitan Trail on the left (GPS: N31 53.47' / W104 49.46'). Go straight.

0.8 Junction with Guadalupe Peak Horse Trail (GPS: N31 53.38' / W104 50.06'). Keep left.

3.2 Guadalupe Peak Backcountry Campground on right. Keep straight.

4.25 Summit of Guadalupe Peak (GPS: N31 53.29' / W104 51.38').

8.5 Arrive back at the trailhead.

Frijole Ranch Trailhead

4 Manzanita Spring Trail

A short ADA-accessible trail to a lush pond and spring near the historic Frijole Ranch.

Distance: 0.75 mile round-trip
Hiking time: 30 minutes
Difficulty: Easy
Elevation gain: Minimal
Type of hike: Out-and-back paved trail
Best seasons: Year-round. Summer days can be hot.
Restrictions: Open year-round with no restrictions. Dogs not allowed. Do not wade or bathe in the springs; it's essential for area wildlife and birds.
Maps: Guadalupe Peak USGS Quad; 203 National Geographic/ Trails Illustrated Guadalupe Mountains National Park Trail Map; park map
Trail contact: Guadalupe Mountains National Park (see appendix)

Finding the trailhead: From the main entrance to Guadalupe National Park (visitor center, campground, and Pine Springs Trailhead), drive east on US 62/180 for 1.4 miles and turn left or north on Frijole Ranch Road. Drive north on the gravel road for 0.6 mile and turn left into a large parking lot with vault toilets, picnic tables covered with ramadas, water, trash and recycling receptacles, and the Frijole Ranch Trailhead on the northeast side of the lot. Trailhead GPS: N31 54.23' / W104 48.05'

The Hike

The 0.35-mile Manzanita Spring Trail is an out-and-back hike on a paved ADA-accessible trail that passes the historic Frijole Ranch and ends at Manzanita Spring, a spring-fed pond surrounded by tall grass. The short trail is part of the longer Smith Spring Trail, which continues past Manzanita Spring as a rough singletrack trail. The trail and The Pinery Trail are the only handicap-accessible trails in the national park. Its paved surface is suitable for wheelchairs and strollers. No shade is found on the trail, except at Frijole Ranch, so carry water and wear a hat and sunscreen on hot days.

Start the hike at the Frijole Ranch Trailhead at the northeast corner of a large parking lot. A trailhead kiosk has a map, park and trail information, and a hiker register. Nearby are vault toilets, water fountains, and picnic tables shaded by ramadas.

The trail heads northeast and joins Frijole Ranch Road, a closed park access road, after 75 feet. It continues along the left side of the gravel road, then crosses it and passes along the western edge of the walled Frijole Ranch History Museum. A right turn after 400 feet leads through a gate to the old ranch headquarters and the museum, which details the national park's human history. Exhibits interpret Native Americans, including the Mescalero Apache, as well as the ranching history, which dates to 1860 when the Rader brothers homesteaded at Frijole and Manzanita springs.

John and Nellie Smith took over the ranch in 1906 after George and Ida Wolcott abandoned it in 1895. The Smiths planted orchards of apple, peach, apricot, plum, and pear trees, grew berries and crops, and raised cattle, pigs, and horses. The ranch buildings seen today were built by the Smith family in the 1920s, including the ranch house, bunkhouse, outhouse, spring house, shed, barn, and a school house to educate their ten children. Frijole Ranch was sold to J.C. Hunter in 1942. After acquiring 67,312 acres, the Hunter family sold the ranch to the National Park Service for $22 an acre in 1966.

The museum is staffed intermittently by volunteers, but the grounds are always open.

The trail makes a sharp right at the northwest corner of the ranch and heads northeast across an open landscape covered with grass, yucca, and shrubs. The high escarpment of the Frijole Ridge, topped by 8,368-foot Hunter Peak on the left, fills the northwestern horizon, while the conical knob of 5,682-foot Nipple Hill rises to the east. After crossing a couple of dry washes, the trail reaches Manzanita Spring and the end of the accessible trail after 0.35 mile (0.2 mile from Frijole Ranch).

Manzanita Spring forms a broad, shallow pond lined with tall grass. The spring is a watering hole for local wildlife and birds. If you visit in early morning or evening you may glimpse mule deer, coyote, and occasionally elk. The spring also offers great habitat for the park's 289 bird species. Summer brings white-throated swifts and violet-green swallows catching insects above the spring. Bring binoculars and a field guide, and pick up a bird checklist at the visitor center to identify different species. Since the spring and the pond are important wildlife habitat in this dry region, protect it by staying on the trail and avoid contaminating the spring water by wading.

The trail abruptly ends on the northwest corner of Manzanita Spring. Able-bodied members of your party can make a short loop hike on a singletrack trail around the lake. Smith Spring Trail continues north from Manzanita Spring for another mile to lush Smith Spring. After admiring the great views and watching wildlife, return on the paved path to the trailhead for a 0.75-mile hike.

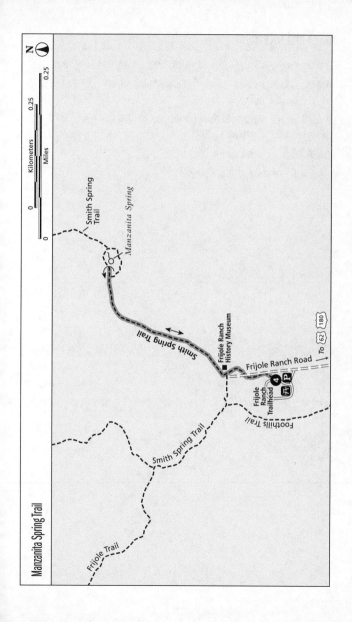

Manzanita Spring Trail

N

Kilometers
0   0.25
Miles
0   0.25

Smith Spring Trail

Manzanita Spring

Smith Spring Trail

Frijole Ranch History Museum

Frijole Ranch Road

To 62 180

Frijole Ranch Trailhead

Foothills Trail

Smith Spring Trail

Frijole Trail

Miles and Directions

0.0   Frijole Ranch Trailhead (GPS: N31 54.23' / W104 48.05').

500 ft   Reach the Frijole Ranch History Museum. Go right on the paved trail.

0.35   Reach Manzanita Spring and end of ADA trail (GPS: N31 54.37' / W104 47.54').

0.7   Return to Frijole Ranch.

0.75   Arrive back at the trailhead.

5 Smith Spring Trail

A moderate hike past an historic ranch, Manzanita Spring, and lush Smith Spring on the southeast flank of the Guadalupe Mountains.

Distance: 2.55 miles. Smith Spring Trail is 2.3 miles long.
Hiking time: 1.5-2 hours
Difficulty: Moderate
Elevation gain: 402 feet
Type of hike: Loop
Best seasons: Year-round. Summer days can be hot.
Restrictions: Open year-round with no restrictions. Dogs not allowed. Do not wade or bathe in the springs; it's essential for area wildlife and birds.
Maps: Guadalupe Peak USGS Quad; National Geographic/Trails Illustrated Guadalupe Mountains National Park Trail Map 203; park map
Trail contact: Guadalupe Mountains National Park (see appendix)

Finding the trailhead: From the main entrance to Guadalupe National Park (visitor center, campground, and Pine Springs Trailhead), drive east on US 62/180 for 1.4 miles and turn left or north on Frijole Ranch Road. Drive north on the gravel road for 0.6 mile and turn left into a large parking lot with vault toilets, picnic tables covered with ramadas, water, trash and recycling receptacles, and the Frijole Ranch Trailhead on the northeast side of the lot. Trailhead GPS: N31 54.23' / W104 48.05'

The Hike

The Smith Spring Trail explores the history, vegetation, wildlife, and geology of the Guadalupe Mountains. The trail offers mountain views, the sound of trickling water, plentiful shade, and birdsong. The 2.3-mile loop hike, and an additional

0.2 mile to and from the trailhead, passes the Frijole Ranch History Museum, Manzanita Spring, and lush Smith Spring, a desert oasis surrounded by thick forest. The first trail section from the parking lot to Manzanita Spring, described in a separate chapter, is an excellent ADA handicap-accessible trail with a hardened surface for wheelchairs and strollers.

The trail, beginning at Frijole Ranch, can be hiked in either direction. The counterclockwise option is described here since it lets you hike the easy section to Manzanita Spring first. To follow the loop trail clockwise, go left or west from the ranch buildings and return on the east side of the loop.

Start the hike at the Frijole Ranch Trailhead on the northeast side of the parking lot. A kiosk at the trailhead has trail and park information, a map, and hiker register. Remember to sign in before hiking. Restrooms, water, and picnic tables shaded by ramadas are at the lot. Follow the paved trail northeast for 500 feet along an access road to the Frijole Ranch History Museum. Smith Spring Trail begins at the north side of the museum, with the east branch on the right and the west branch on the left.

The Frijole Ranch, now a park museum that details the area's history, is a restored homestead first built in 1876 by the Rader brothers near Frijole Spring. The Smith family, which operated the remote ranch beginning in 1906, built most of the current buildings in the 1920s. The working ranch was sold to the National Park Service in 1966. The site includes a ranch house, bunkhouse, outhouse, spring house, shed, barn, and a schoolhouse for the Smith's ten children. The ranch interprets the human history of the Guadalupe Mountains, including early Native Americans, Apaches, and the ranching community. While the grounds are always open with picnic tables beneath shady trees, the museum is open intermittently.

The paved trail heads northeast from the ranch, crossing a couple of dry washes, and after 0.35 mile (0.2 from the ranch) reaches Manzanita Spring and the end of the ADA-accessible trail. The spring forms a shallow pond lined with tall grass and reeds. The spring supplied water to Native Americans as well as the nearby farm. It's also a haven for wildlife and birds, including many of the park's 289 bird species.

Past Manzanita Spring, the trail narrows and bends north. It gently climbs a sloped outwash plain south of the mountains and then follows the edge of Smith Canyon, a dry wash filled with trees. The obvious conical peak to the east is 5,682-foot Nipple Hill. Higher, the trail dips across the wash and traverses stony slopes before entering a woodland surrounding Smith Spring. You reach the spring after hiking 1.3 miles from the trailhead.

Smith Spring is a desert oasis, with cold water tumbling over a small falls into a shady pool. The water, originating from mountain snows and rainfall, seeps down through permeable layers of limestone before emerging below the towering Frijole Ridge. The spring's pond and a small creek, which flows southeast before disappearing beneath streambed cobbles, is surrounded by a dense grove of trees, including Texas madrone, big-toothed maple, ponderosa pine, chinkapin oak, and chokecherry. Ferns, sedge, and moss grow on moist rocks and crevices, creating an idyllic setting in this land of little rain.

The spring attracts wildlife year-round with its perennial water, including deer, elk, coyote, and aoudad or Barbary sheep, an introduced African species, as well as numerous birds. Common birds include chipping and lark sparrows, doves, jays, Say's phoebes, mockingbirds, canyon towhees, warblers, orioles, bluebirds, flickers, woodpeckers,

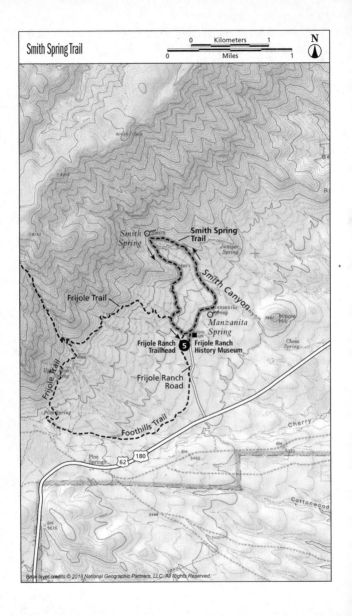

Smith Spring Trail

Smith Spring
Smith Spring Trail
Juniper Spring
Smith Canyon
Frijole Trail
Manzanita Spring
Frijole Ranch Trailhead
5
Frijole Ranch History Museum
Frijole Trail
Frijole Ranch Road
Nipple Hill
Choza Spring
Pine Spring
Foothills Trail
Pine Spring
62 180
BM 5465
BM 5423
Cherry
Cottonwood
BM 5616

hummingbirds, and meadowlarks. Bring binoculars and a field guide to identify species.

Please stay on the trail-side of the spring and pond to protect this important wildlife watering hole. Avoid contact with the water by not wading or splashing in the pond, which contaminates the water.

The trail leaves shaded Smith Spring and climbs out of the shallow canyon onto dry slopes covered with dry scrubs, yuccas, and short grass. The trail heads southwest around a rocky spur, passing sections of loose rock. Look for a section of green rock deposited over 265 million years ago as ash from a volcanic eruption. After crossing a wooded wash, head south to the junction with Frijole Trail at 2.2 miles from the trailhead and 0.9 mile from Smith Spring. Go left at the junction. Hike southeast past the trail's junction with Foothills Trail at 2.4 miles and reach Frijoles Ranch. Go right on the paved trail for 500 feet back to the parking lot.

Miles and Directions

0.0 Frijole Ranch Trailhead (GPS: N31 54.23' / W104 48.05').

500 ft Reach the Frijole Ranch History Museum. Go right on the paved trail.

0.35 Reach Manzanita Spring and end of ADA trail (GPS: N31 54.37' / W104 47.54').

1.3 Reach Smith Spring (GPS: N31 55.06' / W104 48.24').

2.2 Junction with Frijole Trail (GPS: N31 54.33' / W104 48.13'). Go left.

2.4 Junction with Foothills Trail (GPS: N31 54.27' / W104 48.08'). Go left.

2.5 Return to trail at Frijole Ranch.

2.55 Arrive back at the trailhead.

6 Frijole-Foothills Trail Loop

A moderate loop hike on the Foothills and Frijoles trails on slopes between Frijole Ranch and Pine Springs Visitor Center.

Distance: 4.5 miles
Hiking time: 2–3 hours
Difficulty: Moderate
Elevation gain: 160 feet on Foothills Trail; 500 feet on Frijoles Trail
Type of hike: Loop
Best seasons: Year-round. Summer days can be hot.

Restrictions: Open year-round with no restrictions. No dogs allowed.
Maps: Guadalupe Peak USGS Quad; 203 National Geographic/ Trails Illustrated Guadalupe Mountains National Park Trail Map; park map
Trail contact: Guadalupe Mountains National Park (see appendix)

Finding the trailhead: From the main entrance to Guadalupe National Park (visitor center, campground, and Pine Springs Trailhead), drive east on US 62/180 for 1.4 miles and turn left or north on Frijole Ranch Road. Drive north on the gravel road for 0.6 mile and turn left into a large parking lot with vault toilets, picnic tables covered with ramadas, water, trash and recycling receptacles, and the Frijole Ranch Trailhead on the northeast side of the lot. Trailhead GPS: N31 54.23' / W104 48.05'

The Hike

The Foothills and Frijole trails form a good 4.5-mile loop hike between the Frijoles Ranch Trailhead and the Pine Springs Trailhead on a sloping outwash plain below Hunter Peak. The mostly easy hike, following good trails, is seldom busy so you'll usually be alone. Although the hike can be done in either direction, it's best to start the hike from Frijoles

Ranch and hike it clockwise. If you start from Pine Springs Trailhead near the park visitor center and campground, add another 1.1 miles to the round-trip hike distance.

The two-mile Foothills Trail section runs from the Frijoles Ranch historic site to a junction with Frijoles Trail, which connects the Pine Springs Trailhead and Tejas Trail with Smith Spring Trail near Frijoles Ranch. The Frijoles Trail accesses the Tejas Trail, which climbs to the crest of the Guadalupe Mountains by 8,368-foot Hunter Peak and Pine Top Backcountry Campsite, and the strenuous Bear Canyon Trail, which ascends to The Bowl, a unique valley filled with a pine and fir woodland.

This loop hike, like other low-elevation hikes at Guadalupe Mountains National Park, is hot during the summer and little shade is found on the route. Wear a hat and sunscreen and carry plenty of water and sports drinks. Hike it in the early morning or evening for cooler temperatures.

Begin the hike at the Frijole Ranch Trailhead on the northeast side of the parking lot. A trailhead kiosk offers trail and park information, park map, and hiker register. Sign in before hiking. Nearby are restrooms, water, and picnic tables shaded by ramadas. Follow the paved trail northeast for 500 feet along an access road to the Frijole Ranch History Museum. West of the museum are two trails. Foothills Trail is the first one, a short spur leads to the main north-south Foothills Trail. Alternatively, go west from the northwest corner of the ranch to the west trailhead for Smith Spring Trail. Hike a couple 100 feet, then go left on marked Foothills Trail.

The historic Frijole Ranch, a park museum that explains the history of the Guadalupes, is worth visiting before your hike. The ranch is a homestead first settled in 1876 by the Rader brothers. Starting in 1906, the Smith family operated the ranch and built many of the current buildings in the 1920s. The site includes a ranch house, bunkhouse, outhouse, spring hours, shed, barn, and schoolhouse for the Smith's ten children. The museum interprets the area's human history, including early Native Americans, Apaches, and ranchers. The museum is open intermittently depending on staffing, but the shady grounds are always open.

The two-mile Foothills Trail segment of the hike heads south, paralleling the Frijole Ranch Road for 0.8 mile to a trail junction. A 0.12-mile-long spur trail goes left here to a parking lot, restrooms, and stock corral on the road just north of the highway. These trails are open for horseback riding.

The trail bends west, dips across a couple dry washes, and then follows the northern edge of the wide wash that drains out of Pine Spring Canyon. This 1.2-mile trail section parallels US 62/180, with occasional passing traffic to the south.

Foothills Trail gradually bends northwest and after 2 miles it reaches a three-way junction with Frijoles Trail directly north of the Pine Springs Visitor Center. To reach this junction from the Pine Springs Trailhead, the jumping-off point for trails up Guadalupe Peak and to Devil's Hall, hike north on Tejas Trail to a junction on the north side of the broad wash and go right on Frijole Trail. After hiking a half-mile from the trailhead, you'll reach the junction with Foothills Trail. Go north or left on Frijole Trail.

The Frijole Trail segment goes 2.1 miles to a junction with Smith Spring Trail just west of Frijole Ranch. After leaving Foothills Trail, the hike bends north across the mouth of a shallow green valley, which is watered by trickling Pine Spring to the north. It's best not to hike to the spring since it's an important water source for area wildlife and birds.

The trail begins a gradual climb northeast along the base of the mountains, crossing open slopes and dry washes. After 3 miles of hiking from the trailhead or 0.9 mile from the Foothills-Frijole junction, the trail reaches a junction with

Frijole-Foothills Trails Loop

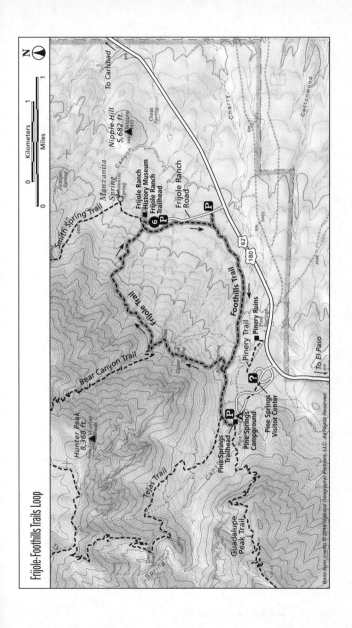

Bear Canyon Trail at about 6,000 feet. The three-mile trail climbs about 2,000 feet up Bear Canyon to the top of the Guadalupe Mountains, joining the Bowl Trail in a cool relict forest behind Hunter Peak at 8,000 feet. Elk and other wildlife roam this remote high-elevation valley.

From Bear Canyon Trail, the hike follows the drainage and then heads northeast across slopes, crossing several more dry washes, before gently descending down to a junction with Smith Spring Trail at 4.2 miles. Go right and follow the trail past the starting junction with Foothills Trail to Frijole Ranch. Visit the ranch or head right down the trail along Frijole Ranch Road to the trailhead and parking lot.

Miles and Directions

0.0   Start at the Frijole Ranch Trailhead (GPS: N31 54.23' / W104 48.05').

0.1   Junction with Foothills Trail/Smith Spring Trail by Frijole Ranch History Museum (GPS: N31 54.27' / W104 48.05'). Go left.

0.15   Three-way trail junction (GPS: N31 54.27' / W104 48.08'). Go left on Foothills Trail.

0.8   Three-way trail junction (GPS: N31 53.56' / W104 48.07'). Keep right. Left spur goes 650 feet to corral parking lot on Frijole Ranch Road.

2.1   Junction with Frijole Trail (GPS: N31 53.52' / W104 49.17'). Go right. A left turn goes 0.55 mile to Pine Springs Trailhead.

3.0   Junction with Bear Canyon Trail (GPS: N31 54.24' / W104 49.06'). Go right across rocky wash.

4.2   Junction with Smith Spring Trail (GPS: N31 54.33' / W104 48.13'). Go right.

4.3   Junction with Foothills Trail. Go straight to Frijole Ranch History Museum.

4.5   Arrive back at the trailhead.

McKittrick Canyon Trailhead

7   McKittrick Canyon Nature Trail

An excellent, family-friendly trail by the McKittrick Canyon Visitor Center that explores the geology and natural history of the Guadalupe Mountains.

Distance: 0.9 mile

Hiking time: 1 hour

Difficulty: Moderately easy

Elevation gain: 214 feet

Type of hike: Lollipop loop

Best seasons: Year-round. Summers are hot.

Restrictions: Day-use only area. All hikers must exit the canyon and park road by closing time. Dogs not allowed.

Maps: Guadalupe Peak USGS Quad; National Geographic Trails/ Illustrated Guadalupe Mountains National Park Trail Map 203; park map

Trail contact: Guadalupe Mountains National Park (see appendix)

Finding the trailhead: From the Pine Springs Visitor Center and campground area, drive northeast on US 62/180 for 8 miles to a signed left turn on McKittrick Road. Follow the paved road for 4.5 miles to the McKittrick Canyon Visitor Center and parking lot. Walk through the visitor center to the trailhead on the north side of the building. Trailhead GPS: N31 58.39' / W104 45.07'

The Hike

The McKittrick Canyon Nature Trail is a 0.9-mile-long singletrack trail that makes a loop hike across a scrubby outwash slope below the Guadalupe Mountains. This excellent kid-friendly hike, lying near the mouth of McKittrick Canyon on the eastern side of the national park, offers lots of interpretive signs that explain the native plants and animals of the Chihuahuan Desert, the area's geology, and wildland fires. The hike is also great for birdwatching, with numerous species found in a valley below the trail. Allow an hour to hike the moderately easy trail.

McKittrick Canyon, including the entrance road, visitor center, and trails is a day-use only area. The area is open from 8 a.m. to 6 p.m. (MDT) from early to mid-March through early November, and from 8 a.m. to 4:30 p.m. (MST) from November to March. Allow enough time to hike the trail so you can leave McKittrick Canyon before the posted closing time. The entrance gate on US 62/180 is locked every evening.

The hike begins on the north side of the McKittrick Canyon Visitor Center. Walk north 50 feet to a trail junction just before a kiosk with park information in English and Spanish, including suggested trails, a hiker's checklist, park map, and park safety tips. There is also a station for filling out a park entrance envelope. At the trail junction, go left on the nature trail.

Follow the trail southwest past the visitor center and reach a Y-junction after 370 feet. Go left at the junction. While the loop section of the trail can be hiked in either direction, this description goes in a clockwise direction.

The narrow trail follows the northern edge of a shallow valley filled with trees and birdsong watered by an intermittent spring. Grasses, yuccas, succulents, cacti, and shrubs line the trail, including barberry, mountain mahogany, and creosote bush. Clusters of prickly pear cacti, one of almost fifty cactus species in the national park, thrive on the warm south-facing slopes beside agaves and yuccas, which grow tall stalks in spring before flowering between April and June. Juniper trees, including alligator juniper, scatter across the valley below the trail.

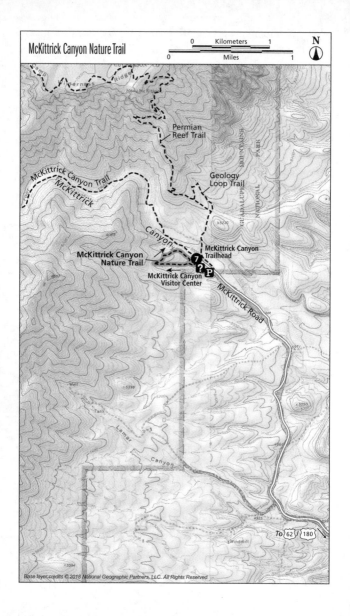

McKittrick Canyon Nature Trail

0 — Kilometers — 1

0 — Miles — 1

N

Permian
Reef Trail

McKittrick Canyon Trail

McKittrick

Canyon

Geology
Loop Trail

McKittrick Canyon
Nature Trail

McKittrick Canyon
Trailhead

7

McKittrick Canyon
Visitor Center

McKittrick Road

To 62 / 180

After 0.4 mile the trail makes a sharp right and climbs northeast for 0.1 mile onto a rounded ridge before bending right and edging along a bluff above the mouth of McKittrick Canyon. The canyon, sometimes called the most beautiful place in Texas, is dominated by mountains and cliffs. Stop on the bluff-top for a drink of water and to read an interpretive sign about the geology of the Capitan Reef to the north, the 2,000-foot limestone face of an underwater reef formed during the Permian Period between 260 and 270 million years ago.

The stony path heads east, gently descending the broad ridge before making a couple switchbacks down to the trail junction at the start of the loop. Go left and hike another 0.1 mile back to the trailhead and visitor center.

Miles and Directions

0.0 Start at the trailhead on the north side of the visitor center.

50 ft Walk to a junction by a kiosk (GPS: N31 58.39' / W104 45.08'). Go left.

0.1 Reach a Y-junction (GPS: N31 58.37' / W104 45.10'). Go left to hike the trail clockwise.

0.4 Reach a sharp right turn at a dry wash (GPS: N31 58.37' / W104 45.30'). Keep right.

0.8 Reach main junction. Go left toward visitor center.

0.9 Arrive back at the trailhead.

8 McKittrick Canyon Trail

An excellent and popular hike on an out-and-back trail alongside a creek bed to historic Pratt Cabin.

Distance: 2.4 miles one-way to Pratt Lodge; 4.8 miles round-trip; 7.2 miles round-trip to The Grotto and Hunter Line Cabin
Hiking time: 4–6 hours
Difficulty: Easy to Pratt Cabin; moderate to The Grotto
Elevation gain: 200 feet to Pratt Cabin
Type of hike: Out-and-back trail
Best seasons: Year-round. Summers can be hot.
Restrictions: Day-use only area. All hikers must exit the canyon and park road by closing time.

Dogs not allowed. No wading, off-trail hiking, camping, or campfires. South McKittrick Canyon is closed past Hunter Line Camp. North McKittrick Canyon is closed past Pratt Cabin.
Maps: Guadalupe Peak USGS Quad; National Geographic Trails/ Illustrated Guadalupe Mountains National Park Trail Map 203; park map
Trail contact: Guadalupe Mountains National Park (see appendix)

Finding the trailhead: From the Pine Springs Visitor Center and campground area, drive northeast on US 62/180 for 8 miles to a signed left turn on McKittrick Road. Follow the paved road for 4.5 miles to the McKittrick Canyon Visitor Center and parking lot. Walk through the visitor center to the trailhead on the north side of the building. Trailhead GPS: N31 58.39' / W104 45.07'

The Hike

The popular McKittrick Canyon Trail is a superb out-and-back adventure up a deep canyon to historic Pratt Cabin. Day hikers can continue another mile to The Grotto and

Hunter's Line Cabin. Here the trail leaves the canyon and steeply climbs to The Notch and McKittrick Ridge, gaining 2,700 feet, on one of the park's toughest trails. The 4.8-mile round-trip hike to Pratt Cabin, however, is easy, family friendly, and has minimal elevation gain.

McKittrick Canyon, considered one of the most beautiful spots in Texas, is a place of running water and shady trees. It's particularly gorgeous in late October and early November when autumn paints the maples and oaks with a palette of red, yellow, and orange. The canyon formed the nucleus of Guadalupe National Park, when geologist Wallace E. Pratt donated 4,988 acres in McKittrick Canyon to the National Park Service around 1960. Pratt had wandered up the creek in 1921 and called it "the most beautiful spot I'd ever seen." He bought up the canyon, had a stone cabin built, and spent summers there until the 1950s.

The wide trail mostly follows an old road to Pratt Cabin, with only a singletrack section at the beginning. It has a gentle gradient with 200 feet of elevation gain from the trailhead to the cabin. A spring-fed, perennial creek flows in a few sections of the canyon, but it disappears among cobbles. Do not drink or wade in the stream since animals depend on its meager flow, including a small population of trout. Wading alters the water's temperature and can kill aquatic life.

McKittrick Canyon, named for 1870s rancher Felix McKittrick, is a day-use only area to protect its fragile ecosystems and wilderness qualities. The canyon area is open daily from 8 a.m. to 6 p.m. (MDT) from early to mid-March through early November, and 8 a.m. to 4:30 p.m. (MST) from November to March. Hikers must leave the canyon before closing time. An entrance gate on McKittrick Road at US 62/180 is locked at night. No camping, fires, pets, or hiking off the trail is allowed in the canyon.

Begin the hike at the small interpretive center, which is usually open during the day. The center offers restrooms, water, and informative displays about the canyon's unique geology, history, and natural history, and tips on desert hiking and safety. Make sure to fill your water bottles at a tap on the north side of the building. Walk through an open breezeway in the center and descend a ramp to the trailhead and a kiosk with a hiker sign-out register and a station to pay your park entrance fee. The McKittrick Nature Trail goes left at the kiosk.

The trail heads northwest on a bench above the wide, stony wash at the mouth of McKittrick Canyon, and after 0.25 mile descends down to sandstone slabs and the creek bed. The creek is usually dry here, but water sometimes trickles along the bed after rain. Cross the creek and continue northwest on the singletrack trail and reach a junction with an old closed road at the 0.45-mile mark. Go left on the doubletrack trail.

The trail goes west, following the dry creek bed as it makes several wide bends on the canyon floor beneath steep brushy mountain slopes. In a couple places the water emerges from the rounded cobbles in the creek bed, pooling beneath trees and tumbling over small boulders. When Wallace Pratt first visited and lived in the canyon, the creek flowed year-round along its length. He described its beauty as "a sparkling succession of miniature lakes and waterfalls . . . closely bordered by lush green growth . . . bounded by gray walls towering under the blue desert sky." Huge flash floods in 1943 and 1968, however, destroyed travertine dams, ponds, waterfalls, and plant life, and forced the steam underground.

As you head west on the trail, observe the changing vegetation. The first part of the hike passes through a typical

Chihuahuan Desert ecosystem with creosote bush, lechuguilla, sotol, ocotillo, and soaptree yucca. Farther west a ribbon of trees lines the water course, providing shade and shelter for animals and humans. Rough bark, checkered like alligator skin, covers twisted alligator junipers. Velvet ashes, big-tooth maples, gray oaks, and even occasional ponderosa pines, far below their normal elevation, shade the path and thickets of prickly pear cacti and agave. The Texas madrone is perhaps the prettiest tree, with its smooth, red bark and scented spring flowers. This southern tree rarely grows north of here.

The canyon slowly narrows, with steep slopes dense with thick brush and broken by limestone cliffs overlooking the wooded canyon floor. After crossing the creek bed for the seventh time, the trail reaches a trail junction at 2.35 miles. Go right on a side trail, passing through a gateway, and walk up a cobble stone path to the historic Pratt Cabin, the 2.4-mile end point and turn-around spot for this hike.

The house, sitting on a broad bench above the confluence of North and South McKittrick Canyons, was the seasonal home for Wallace Pratt and his family from the early 1930s until the 1950s. Construction on the stone and wood house began in the winter of 1931–1932. Pratt selected the fine-grained stone from an exposure in the creek bed near today's visitor center, while the pine rafters and beams were hauled from east Texas. Pratt, a geologist and oilman with Humble Oil (which later became Exxon), spent summers at the isolated house. He became a conservationist during those decades and eventually donated his Guadalupe land as the seed for the national park, which was established in 1966.

Now the Stone Cabin, as Pratt called it, includes several outbuildings, a stone picnic table, and a fence of piled

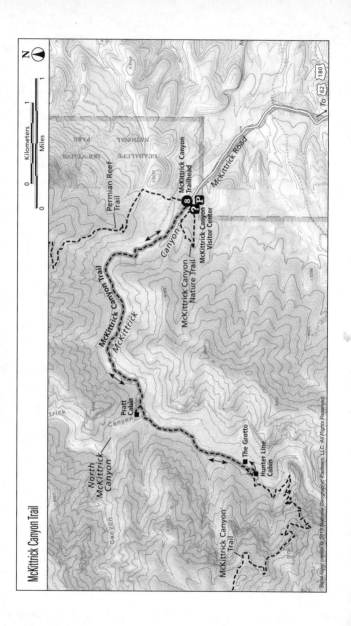

McKittrick Canyon Trail

stones that are preserved as a historic site that's listed on the National Register of Historic Places. The cabin includes a large living room, bedroom, kitchen, bathroom, and kitchen. It's occasionally open if a ranger is present there. Otherwise, hikers are welcome to relax on chairs on the shady front porch and enjoy the scenery and solitude.

After exploring the cabin and its grounds, return to the main trail and go left to retrace your steps back to the visitor center and parking lot. Intrepid hikers can also continue west on McKittrick Canyon Trail for another 1.1 miles through thick forest above the north side of the creek bed to a side trail that leads to The Grotto and the Hunter Line Cabin in South McKittrick Canyon. The Grotto is a unique surface shelter cave filled with speleothems like stalactites. The Hunter Line Cabin was quarters for cowboys that worked on the Guadalupe Mountains Ranch.

South McKittrick Canyon past the cabin is closed to all visitors. It's preserved as a natural area for wildlife and its pristine ecosystems. The McKittrick Canyon Trail continues above the cabin, switchbacking up steep slopes to The Notch at 6,045 feet and a backcountry campsite at the top of McKittrick Ridge at 7,716 feet, 2,300 feet above the canyon floor. This hike is best done by backpackers, who can continue west on the trail to the Tejas Trail, which leads north to Dog Canyon Trailhead or south to Pine Springs Trailhead by the main visitor center.

Miles and Directions

0.0	Begin at trailhead at rear of visitor center.
50 ft	Walk to junction and kiosk (GPS: N31 58.39' / W104 45.08'). Continue straight on the trail.
0.25	Reach creek crossing (GPS: N31 58.47' / W104 45.21').

0.45 Junction with closed road/trail (GPS: N31 58.53' / W104 45.26'). Go left on doubletrack trail.

2.35 Junction with Pratt Cabin trail (GPS: N31 58.59' / W104 46.47'). Go right and hike uphill to Pratt Cabin.

2.4 End of trail at Pratt Cabin (GPS: N31 59.01' / W104 46.50'). Return to main trail and go left or east.

4.8 Arrive back at the trailhead.

Trail to The Grotto and Hunter Line Cabin

0.0 Pratt Cabin trail junction. Go right or southwest on McKittrick Canyon Trail.

1.1 Reach a junction with a spur trail on the left (GPS: N31 58.14' / W104 47.17'). Go left to The Grotto.

1.15 The Grotto (GPS: N31 58 12' / W104 47.17').

1.2 Hunter Line Cabin (GPS: N31 58.10' / W104 47.19').

2.4 Return to Pratt Cabin junction.

7.2 Go straight for 2.4 miles to the visitor center and parking lot for a 7.2-mile round-trip hike from the trailhead at the visitor center.

$\mathcal{9}$ Permian Reef Trail

An excellent hike up a strenuous trail with interpretive geology markers to a high ridge with spectacular views across the national park.

Distance: 3 miles one-way to ridge top; 6 miles round-trip; 4.6 miles one-way to park boundary
Hiking time: 6–8 hours
Difficulty: Strenuous
Elevation gain: 2,000 feet
Type of hike: Out-and-back trail
Best seasons: Oct to May. Summer days are hot on the exposed trail.
Restrictions: Day-use only area, except for backcountry campsite on upper trail. All hikers must exit the canyon and park road by closing time. No dogs allowed.
Maps: Guadalupe Peak USGS Quad; National Geographic Trails/Illustrated Guadalupe Mountains National Park Trail Map 203; park map
Trail contact: Guadalupe Mountains National Park (see appendix)

Finding the trailhead: From the Pine Springs Visitor Center and campground area, drive northeast on US 62/180 for 8 miles to a signed left turn on McKittrick Road. Follow the paved road for 4.5 miles to the McKittrick Canyon Visitor Center and parking lot. Walk through the visitor center to the trailhead on the north side of the building. Trailhead GPS: N31 58.39' / W104 45.07'

The Hike

The Permian Reef Trail, climbing 2,000 feet from the McKittrick Canyon Visitor Center to Camp Wilderness Ridge, ascends the south face of Capitan Reef, an ancient fossil reef from the Permian geologic period over 260 million years ago. The strenuous trail, climbing 3 miles to a high ridge and 4.6 miles to the park's northern boundary, offers not only marvelous views into deep McKittrick Canyon but also allows geologists and students the opportunity to study the reef's fossils and rock formations.

Before doing the hike, pick up *The Permian Reef Trail Guide*, a free 14-page booklet available at the park visitor center that details fourteen key geological points on the trail. The trail markers explain the story of Capitan Reef and highlight various fossils and geologic features, helping hikers understand the unique reef. For more information, check at the visitor center for a loaner copy of the interpretive out-of-print guidebook *Listening to the Rocks: A Young Person's Guide to the Permian Reef Trail*. Geologists should use *The Guide to the Permian Reef Geology Trail*, a technical online book published by the Texas Bureau of Economic Geology, which interprets thirty geologic points.

As you hike, remember that all fossils and rock formations are protected in Guadalupe Mountains National Park. Do not remove or damage any fossils, rocks, plants, or any other natural feature.

The Permian Reef Trail is a strenuous hike up a single-track trail that steadily climbs uphill from the trailhead at the mouth of McKittrick Canyon to the 7,000-foot-high ridge above. While this hike description ends on the ridge line near McKittrick point, the trail continues another 1.6 miles across the broad forested ridge, passing Wilderness Ridge Backcountry Campsite, to the national park boundary where the trail continues into Lincoln National Forest in New Mexico.

The Permian Reef Trail is exposed and sunny with almost no shade found along the path until the pine forest atop the ridge. It's best to hike the route between October and April when temperatures are cooler than the hot summer months. Carry plenty of water since none is found on the trail. A gallon per person for a long day's hike is not too much if it's hot. Also, bring sports drinks or packets of electrolytes to replace essential minerals and salt lost by perspiration, and wear a hat and sunscreen. The hike is not recommended for young children because of its steepness, length, and difficulty.

Allow six to eight hours to hike the trail and stop at each geologic marker. It's best to begin in the morning to make sure you have enough time to reach the rim and return to your vehicle before the road closes. The trail and McKittrick Canyon is a day-use only area to protect its ecosystems and wilderness qualities. The area is open daily from 8 a.m. to 6 p.m. (MDT) from early to mid-March through early November, and 8 a.m. to 4:30 p.m. (MST) from November to March. Hikers must leave the area before closing time. An entrance gate on McKittrick Road at US 62/180 is locked at night. If you're locked in after hours, instructions are posted at McKittrick Canyon Visitor Center to have the gate opened.

Start the hike at the small visitor center at the end of McKittrick Canyon Road. The center, usually open during the day, has restrooms, water, and displays about the area's geology, natural history, and human history, and tips on desert hiking and safety. Fill your water bottles at a tap on the north side of the building. Walk through an open breezeway in the building and descend a ramp to the trailhead and a kiosk with a hiker sign-out register and a station to pay your park entrance fee. A three-way trail junction is at the kiosk, with McKittrick Canyon Nature Trail to the left and McKittrick Canyon Trail going straight. Go right on the Permian Reef Trail.

The trail descends a short hill and after 0.05 mile reaches an old road. Go left and follow the road across a wide wash at the mouth of McKittrick Canyon. Climb out of the wash and reach a trail junction after 0.15 mile. Go right on the singletrack Permian Ridge Trail.

The trail heads up barren slopes to a blunt ridge and at 0.4 mile reaches a junction with a geology loop trail, a mile-long path used by geologists and classes. Make a sharp left and follow the main trail for another 0.2 mile to the junction at the end of the geology loop. The trail continues straight, passing below a low cliff band composed of Lamar limestone. After marker 4, it goes through a narrow, shady slot called The Grottos, which was formed when parts of the cliff slumped downhill. This is a good spot to stop for a drink and to cool down in the best shade on the trail.

Past the cliffs, the trail ascends a couple big switchbacks and then heads steadily uphill across open slopes covered with typical Chihuahuan Desert plants, including cholla and prickly pear cacti, agave, sotol, yucca, creosote bush, and small scattered junipers. Keep your interpretive brochure handy to identify the fossils seen at the designated markers, including sponges, bryozoans, and ammonoids. After crossing several steep drainages, the trail passes beneath a towering limestone cliff that formed the face of the massive reef.

The Guadalupe Mountains, stretching southwest from Carlsbad Caverns National Park to Guadalupe Mountains National Park, are part of the huge Permian Reef Complex that formed along the edge of an inland sea in the Delaware Basin over 260 million years ago. The Capitan Reef, form-ing the mountain wall climbed by the Permian Reef Trail, separated a shallow lagoon to the northwest from the deeper water in the sea. Marine life, including algae, clams, coral,

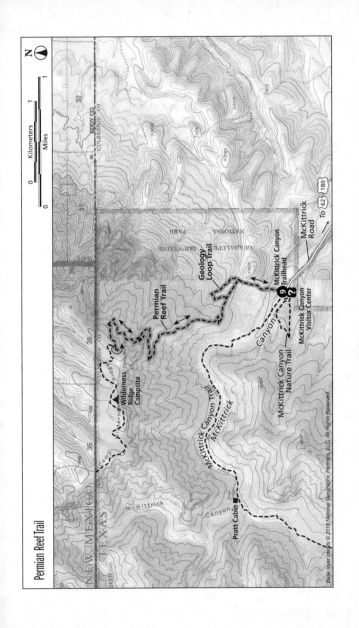

Permian Reef Trail

trilobites, sponges, and sea urchins, filled the sea, with their fossilized remains, lime secretions, and sediment forming the reef's limestone. Geologists visit here to study one of the best examples of a shelf-edge reef in the world.

The trail makes a big switchback right and crosses steep slopes below the big cliff to its right side where it scrambles across bedrock and traverses onto the east side of a ridge. The trail continues rising and switchbacks left to the airy clifftop and then heads up right across three drainages. Finish by cutting back left and threading through sharp cliff bands to the rounded summit of Camp Wilderness Ridge at 3 miles. The described hike ends at boulders on the ridgeline and some of the best views in the park. After sipping water and eating lunch, put your shoes back on and retrace your steps back down the trail for a six-mile, round-trip hike.

For a stunning overlook above twisting McKittrick Canyon, scramble southwest along a social trail on the crest of the ridge for 600 feet to the rocky summit of 6,064-foot McKittrick point. If you have time, you can earn extra credit by following the trail for another 1.6 miles to the national park boundary on the New Mexico border. This excellent and easy trail section crosses low hills shaded by tall ponderosa pines and passes a couple spectacular viewpoints. The Wilderness Ridge Backcountry Campsite, with five separate sites, is 0.7 mile from the hike end point. This scenic area makes a great overnight stopover. At the New Mexico border, the trail becomes the Camp Wilderness Ridge Trail and heads northwest along the ridge for 2.1 miles to a trailhead on FR 3008 in Lincoln National Forest.

Miles and Directions

0.0 Walk 50 feet from the visitor center to the trailhead (GPS: N31 58.39' / W104 45.08') at a kiosk and thee-way trail junction. Go right on Permian Reef Trail.

0.05 Reach a trail junction. Go left on a closed road.

0.15 Reach a trail junction north of a wash (GPS: N31 58.45' / W104 45.06'). Go right on Permian Reef Trail.

0.4 Trail makes sharp left turn at start of geology loop trail (GPS: N31 58.59' / W104 45.01'). Go left on main trail.

0.6 Upper junction with geology loop trail. Continue straight.

0.7 Reach the shaded Grottos (GPS: N31 59.05' / W104 45.16').

1.9 Cross limestone slabs (GPS: N31 59.37' / W104 45.27') on right side of big cliff.

2.2 Top of a ridge with views west into McKittrick Canyon.

3.0 Top of Camp Wilderness Ridge (GPS: N31 59.53' / W104 45.33') and end of the hike.

6.0 Arrive back at the trailhead.

Salt Basin Dunes Trailhead

10 Salt Basin Dunes Trail

A level trail to a large gypsum dune field in the Salt Basin in western Guadalupe Mountains National Park.

Distance: 2.6–4 miles
Hiking time: 1–3 hours
Difficulty: Moderately easy
Elevation gain: Minimal on trail; 60 feet in dunes
Type of hike: Out-and-back
Best seasons: Sept to May. Summers are hot and no shade is found in the area. High winds scour the area in winter and spring.

Restrictions: Dogs not allowed. No camping at parking lot.
Maps: PX Flat and Linda Lake North USGS Quads; park map; National Geographic Trails/ Illustrated Guadalupe Mountains National Park Trail Map 203; park map
Trail contact: Guadalupe Mountains National Park (see appendix)

Finding the trailhead: The trailhead parking lot, located on the western boundary of the national park, is 47 miles from Pine Springs Visitor Center. Drive west from the visitor center and campground on US 62/180 for 23 miles to Salt Flat. Turn right on FM Road 1576 and drive north for 17 miles to William's Road. Turn right on the dirt road and drive 7.5 miles east to the parking lot and trailhead. This road surface is clay and becomes slippery and dangerous after rain. Do not drive if it's wet. The speed limit is 25 miles per hour. Watch for livestock on the road. Gas and food is available in Dell City west of the parking area. Trailhead GPS: N31 55.25' / W105 00.22'

The Hike

The Salt Basin Dunes Trail explores the northern edge of the second largest gypsum sand dune field in the United States. A 2.6-mile round-trip hike goes from the trailhead on the

Guadalupe Mountains National Park's western boundary to the historic Butterfield Stage Route on the north side of the dunes. Hikers can make a half-mile loop through the dunes, following social trails and crossing the open dunes, from the end of the trail. The doubletrack trail follows a level closed road to the stage route.

The Salt Basin Dunes lie at 3,640 feet, about 5,000 feet lower than Guadalupe Peak to the east. While temperatures are pleasant in winter and spring, the area is often scoured by high winds. The summer months are hot, with temperatures often climbing above 100°F. It's best to hike early in the morning. Wear a hat and sunscreen, and carry water. A gallon per person per day is not too much. Heavy thunderstorms, particularly in summer, can make the clay access road slippery and impassable for months. If a storm is brewing, it's best to high-tail it back to your vehicle and drive out before the rain comes. Rattlesnakes are sometimes encountered in the dune field. Keep your distance and walk away from the snake.

A black cryptogamic soil crust covers much of the sandy soil both in the dunes and in the surrounding area. This unique desert soil, composed of lichen and fungi, prevents wind erosion and stabilizes the soil for vegetation. The crypto crust is fragile and damaged by walking on it, which creates erosion. Avoid busting the crust by staying on the established trail from the parking area, and then follow only existing trails into the dunes, and hiking on non-vegetated dunes.

William's Road, the access road from the west, ends at a fence and short loop with parking, restrooms, and two picnic tables shaded by a metal ramada inside the park's west boundary. There is no camping or overnight parking at the lot. The trailhead is on the east side of the parking loop.

A shaded kiosk at the trailhead offers interpretive panels about the geology and natural history of the sand dunes and a station to pay the daily entrance fee.

The trail heads east from the parking area on a closed road. The three highest peaks in Texas—8,751-foot Guadalupe Peak, 8,615-foot Shumard Peak, and 8,631-foot Bush Mountain—line the eastern horizon above the flat Salt Basin. The sand dunes are not visible from the trailhead. Hike east on the straight road for 0.3 mile to a closed parking area. The trail bends left and heads northeast across arid terrain punctuated by scattered bushes and cryptogamic soil along the northern edge of the gleaming white dune field.

A junction with a small trail is at 1.1 miles. This narrow path goes southeast into the dunes. This is the return trail for the described hike into the dunes, although you can follow it onto the low dunes. Continue hiking on the main double-track trail for another 0.2 mile to a major junction with the Butterfield Stage Route trail. A good trail heads southeast here for 350 feet to the base of the highest dunes. Follow the path and don't step on the crypto crust.

After slogging through deep sand, climb the face of the highest dunes and enter a magical white world of barren sand. The white sand dunes are composed of grains of crystalline gypsum that spread across 2,000 acres on the eastern side of the Salt Basin. The northern edge of the dune field forms a mile-long, crescent-shaped ridge of shifting, 60-foot-high sand dunes like those found at the famous White Sands in central New Mexico. The field trends southwest for about 5 miles, with the smaller southern dunes, as low as 3 feet high, anchored by wiry vegetation.

It's easy to wander around the dunes. Hike east across the barren dunes for a half-mile and then descend the dunes

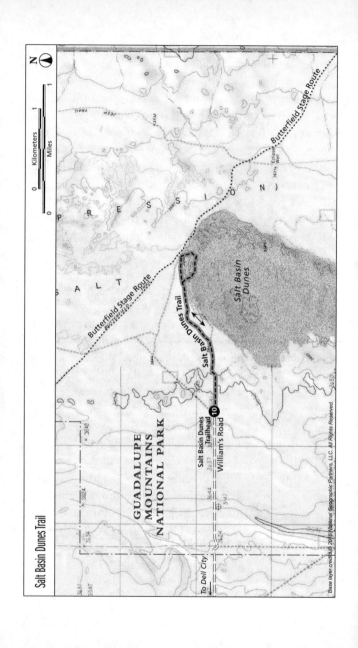

Salt Basin Dunes Trail

to the old stage route and follow it back west to dunes trail. A good hike heads southwest along sand ridges for a third of a mile before picking up the first trail into the dunes and following it 400 feet northwest to the Salt Basin Dunes Trail. Keep a sharp eye out so you can pick up the trail on the north edge of the dunes so you don't bust the crypto crust.

While the dunes appear inhospitable to life, there are plenty of animals, birds, and reptiles that live here. Look for the sidewinding track of a rattlesnake on a dune slope or the tail mark of a lizard. The rare lesser earless lizard lives here, as well as kangaroo rats, pocket mice, kit foxes, and coyotes. Plants anchor the dunes, especially in the southern part of the dune field. Yuccas, often half-buried in sand, rise above the white sands. Many rare plants live among the dunes, including twenty-five endemic species found nowhere else in the world.

After exploring the northern dunes, return to Salt Basin Dunes Trail and follow it west to the trailhead and parking area. Hike distances range from 2 to 4 miles depending on how much you hike around the dune field.

Miles and Directions

0.0   Trailhead at parking lot on William's Road (GPS: N31 55.25' / W105 00.22').

0.3   End of straight road, trail bends left (GPS: N31 55.24' / W105 00.05').

1.1   Junction with trail on right to dunes (GPS: N31 55.38' / W104 59.20'). Continue straight.

1.3   Junction with Butterfield Stage trail and turn-around point (GPS: N31 55.39' / W104 59.07').

2.6   Arrive back at the trailhead.

Dog Canyon Trailhead

11 Indian Meadow Nature Trail

A short nature trail that makes a loop around a wide, grassy meadow once used as a campsite by the Mescalero Apache.

Distance: 0.7 mile
Hiking time: 30 minutes–1 hour
Difficulty: Easy
Elevation gain: Minimal
Type of hike: Lollipop loop
Best seasons: Year-round. Summer days are hot.
Restrictions: Dogs not allowed

Maps: Guadalupe Peak USGS Quad; National Geographic Trails/Illustrated Guadalupe Mountains National Park Trail Map 203; park map
Trail contact: Call the Dog Canyon Visitor Center at (575) 981-2418. Guadalupe Mountains National Park (see appendix)

Finding the trailhead: From Carlsbad, New Mexico, drive north on US 285 for 12 miles. Turn left or west on NM 137 and drive 58 miles to Dog Canyon Visitor Center and Campground just south of the New Mexico border. Park in front of the visitor center and walk 100 feet down the road to the marked trailhead on the left or east side of the road. Trailhead GPS: N31 59.45' / W104 49.58'.

Alternatively, from Pine Springs Visitor Center drive 46 miles northeast on US 52/180 to County Road 408/Dark Canyon Road. Turn left and follow Road 408 for 23 miles to New Mexico 137. Turn left on route 137 and drive 33 miles to the Dog Canyon Visitor Center.

The Hike

The Indian Meadow Nature Trail makes a lollipop loop across a broad meadow west of the Dog Canyon Visitor Center near the northern edge of Guadalupe Mountains National Park by the New Mexico border. The easy 0.6-mile-long trail is mostly level, making it a great hike for families. It's also a good evening or early morning hike since it is right by the Dog Canyon Campground, a quiet camping area with nine tent sites and four RV sites.

The trail is in the Upper Dog Canyon area of the park, a remote valley reached by driving over 100 miles from Pine Springs on the park's southern boundary. The wide canyon at the campground, visitor center, and trail lies at 6,300 feet, making it a cooler and less windy alternative to the Pine Springs area. Wildlife is often seen along the trail, including elk, deer, mountain lion, and turkey.

Begin the hike by parking at a small lot in front of the visitor center, and walk 100 feet south on gravel Dog Canyon Road to the trailhead on the left. The trailhead is a couple hundred feet north of Dog Canyon Campground. The singletrack trail heads east, dipping across a dry arroyo filled with white cobbles. After 320 feet or 0.07 mile, the trail reaches a Y-junction and the start of the loop trail on the western edge of Indian Meadow. Go left or clockwise on the loop.

Early settlers named the area Indian Meadow because the broad grassy meadow was a favorite campsite for the Mescalero Apache or Nde people, who roamed over the sacred land that is today's national park. Dog Canyon Spring south of the trail and campground is one of the few year-round water sources here, making it an important area for the Apache. Evidence of their passage is found at flaking sites where projectile points were made, ring middens used for baking succulent plants like agave, and rock art sites.

The trail makes a 0.6-mile loop around the edge of the broad meadow. A long ridgeline, broken by limestone cliff bands, towers over 1,000 feet above the trail to the east. This ridge forms the western rim of rugged North McKittrick

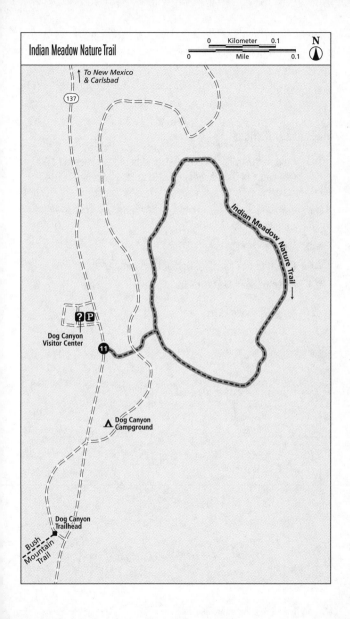

Indian Meadow Nature Trail

0   Kilometer   0.1

0   Mile   0.1

N

↑ To New Mexico
   & Carlsbad

137

Indian Meadow Nature Trail →

? P

Dog Canyon
Visitor Center

11

▲ Dog Canyon
   Campground

■ Dog Canyon
   Trailhead

Bush
Mountain
Trail

Canyon and Devils Den Canyon. As you hike, look for native plants like alligator juniper, ponderosa pine, prickly pear, and cholla cacti.

The trail returns to the Y-junction after 0.62 mile. Go left to return to the trailhead on the road.

Miles and Directions

0.0 Start at the trailhead on the east side of the park road 100 feet south of the visitor center (GPS: N31 59.45' / W104 49 58').

0.07 Walk to a trail junction (GPS: N31 59.46' / W104 49 55'). Go left.

0.2 Trail bends right.

0.62 Return to trail junction. Go left toward road.

0.7 Arrive back at the trailhead.

12 Bush Mountain Trail to Marcus Overlook

A pleasant half-day, out-and-back hike on the Bush Mountain Trail to Marcus Overlook above West Dog Canyon.

Distance: 5 miles
Hiking time: 3–4 hours
Difficulty: Moderate
Elevation gain: 890 feet
Type of hike: Out-and-back
Best seasons: Year-round. Summers are hot. Route has little shade.
Restrictions: Dogs not allowed

Maps: Guadalupe Peak USGS Quad; National Geographic Trails/Illustrated Guadalupe Mountains National Park Trail Map 203; park map
Trail contact: Call the Dog Canyon Visitor Center at (575) 981-2418. Guadalupe Mountains National Park (see appendix)

Finding the trailhead: From Carlsbad, New Mexico, drive north on US 285 for 12 miles. Turn left or west on NM 137 and drive 58 miles to Dog Canyon Visitor Center and Campground just south of the New Mexico border. Continue past the campground on the gravel road to a loop at its end and a large parking lot. The trailhead for Tejas and Bush Mountain trails is at the southwest corner of the lot at a kiosk with park information, map, hiker register, and entrance fee pay station. Trailhead GPS: N31 59.7' / W104 50.02'

Alternatively, from Pine Springs Visitor Center drive 46 miles northeast on US 52/180 to County Road 408/Dark Canyon Road. Turn left and follow Road 408 for 23 miles to New Mexico 137. Turn left on route 137 and drive 33 miles to Dog Canyon Trailhead.

The Hike

The Bush Mountain Trail to Marcus Overlook is a fine half-day hike on the northern edge of Guadalupe Mountains National Park. The moderate route follows a shallow canyon and then climbs onto high rounded ridges that offer great views across the crest of the mountains and north to New Mexico. The out-and-back hike is best done in the cooler months rather than summer since little shade is found along the trail. The singletrack trail is easy to follow but rocky in places. A strong westerly wind often blows on the upper part of the trail, especially in the winter and spring months.

The 11-mile Bush Mountain Trail, one of the park's longest trails, is usually combined with other trails to form an overnight trip from either the Dog Canyon or Pine Springs Trailheads. The trail forms an open loop from Dog Canyon Trailhead to a junction with Tejas Trail, passing over 8,631-foot Bush Mountain. The trail is easily combined with Blue Ridge Trail to Tejas Trail or with Marcus Trail and Tejas Trail for long day hikes from Dog Canyon.

Begin at the Dog Canyon Trailhead at the end of the park road and opposite picnic tables and horse corrals. Farther north on the road is a small visitor center and Dog Canyon Campground, with nine tent sites and four RV sites. This remote trailhead, lying at 6,300 feet, is over 100 road miles from the Pine Springs Visitor Center but only 7 miles as the crow flies. This area of the national park is quiet, uncrowded, and less windy than Pine Springs to the south.

A kiosk at the trailhead offers national park information, a map, hiking safety info, and a hiker register. Pay the park entrance fee here before heading out. The first hike segment follows the Tejas Trail. Head southwest past a maintenance building and cross a grassy meadow and wash to a junction with Bush Mountain Trail at 0.25 mile. Go right on Bush Mountain Trail.

Hike west on the narrow trail through meadows alongside a dry wash in an unnamed canyon. As the canyon pinches down, look for Texas madrone trees along the trail. The red bark on the trees peels to reveal smooth white bark. The tree, a relict left from wetter times, grows as tall as 30 feet, has white flowers clustered at the ends of branches, and gets red fruits that look like small apples, giving it the Spanish name Manzanita. Rough-barked alligator juniper also scatters along the trail.

After 0.9 mile, the trail leaves the stony wash, bends south, and begins slowly ascending a wide ridge. This is open country covered with bunches of grass, scattered junipers, yucca, and agave. Small trees only grow in shallow ravines below the trail. Follow the path along broad Manzanita Ridge until it passes south of a 7,242-foot high point and stop at broken rocks just past two solitary junipers after hiking 2.5 miles.

This spot, Marcus Overlook, is the turn-around point for the hike. Past here the trail begins sharply descending west into West Dog Canyon where it joins Marcus Trail at the wash below and reaches Marcus Backcountry Campsite. This is a good stop for lunch and water if the wind isn't blowing. The views to the west include the Brokeoff Mountains with 6,663-foot Coyote Mountain and Cutoff Ridge on the western edge of the Guadalupe Mountains, while Bush Mountain, the second highest peak in the national park, rises to the southwest.

After enjoying the views and solitude, retrace the trail east to the trailhead for a five-mile, round-trip hike.

Bush Mountain Trail to Marcus Overlook

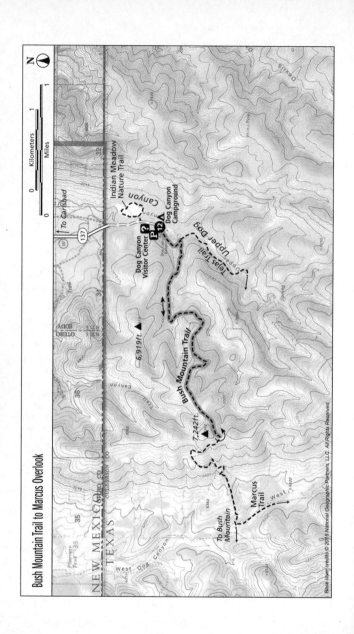

Miles and Directions

0.0 Start at the Dog Canyon Trailhead. (GPS: N31 59.37' / W104 50.02').

0.25 Junction with Bush Mountain Trail (GPS: N31 59.28' / W104 50.08'). Go right.

0.9 Begin climbing away from wash on grassy slopes.

2.5 Turn around point at rocks (GPS: N31 59.11' / W104 51.43').

5.0 Arrive back at the trailhead.

13 Tejas Trail to Lost Peak

An excellent half-day hike that follows a canyon and ridge to the rounded summit of 7,830-foot Lost Peak in the northern part of the national park.

Distance: 6.1 miles round-trip
Hiking time: 4–5 hours
Difficulty: Moderately strenuous
Elevation gain: 1,540 feet
Type of hike: Out-and-back
Best seasons: Year-round. Summers are hot.
Restrictions: Dogs not allowed

Maps: Guadalupe Peak USGS Quad; National Geographic Trails/Illustrated Guadalupe Mountains National Park Trail Map 203; park map
Trail contact: Call the Dog Canyon Visitor Center at (575) 981-2418. Guadalupe Mountains National Park (see appendix)

Finding the trailhead: From Carlsbad, New Mexico, drive north on US 285 for 12 miles. Turn left or west on NM 137 and drive 58 miles to Dog Canyon Visitor Center and Campground just south of the New Mexico border. Continue past the campground on the gravel road to a loop at its end and a large parking lot. The trailhead for Tejas and Bush Mountain trails is at the southwest corner of the lot at a kiosk with park information, map, hiker register, and entrance fee pay station. Trailhead GPS: N31 59.37' / W104 50.02'

Alternatively, from Pine Springs Visitor Center drive 46 miles northeast on US 52/180 to County Road 408/Dark Canyon Road. Turn left and follow Road 408 for 23 miles to New Mexico 137. Turn left on route 137 and drive 33 miles to Dog Canyon Trailhead.

The Hike

The Upper Dog Canyon area in northern Guadalupe Mountains National Park is remote, quiet, and rarely visited when compared to the park's front country to the south. Two long-distance trails—Tejas and Bush Mountain trails—begin at the Dog Canyon Trailhead and run south along the spine of the mountains. One of the best hikes in the northern sector follows Tejas Trail for 3.1 miles to the summit of 7,830-foot Lost Peak, an unranked mountain that offers dramatic views of canyons, cliffs, and peaks.

The Tejas Trail, the main north-to-south path through the national park, runs 11.9 miles from the Dog Canyon Trailhead near the New Mexico border to the Pine Springs Trailhead by the visitor center and campground off US 62/180 below the range's southern escarpment. While Tejas Trail is done as a long day hike or a two-day backpacking trip, most hikers use it as part of a multiday loop hike to McKittrick Canyon, The Bowl, or the Bush Mountain Trail rather than making a lengthy vehicle shuttle between trailheads.

This 6.2-mile out-and-back hike makes a fine half-day excursion through Upper Dog Canyon to a blunt ridge that climbs to Lost Peak's rounded summit. The lower trail traverses an open woodland of alligator juniper, ponderosa pine, Texas madrone, bigtooth maple, and chinkapin oak in the canyon. It's particularly splendid with autumn colors in October and early November. The upper trail crosses scrubby terrain with little shade, so bring plenty of water, wear a hat and sunscreen, and get an early start in summer. It can be windy on the mountain top in winter and spring.

Start the hike at the Dog Canyon Trailhead at the end of the road into Upper Dog Canyon. A small visitor center and the Dog Canyon Campground, with nine tent sites and four RV sites, are just north of the trailhead at 6,300 feet. This remote outpost near the national park's northern boundary is reached by driving over 100 miles from the Pine Springs Visitor Center on the south side of the Guadalupe Mountains. The area, protected by high ridges to the west, is less windy and cooler than the Pine Springs area.

Stop at a trailhead kiosk for national park information, including a map, trails, and hiking safety, and sign out at the hiker register. Also pay the park entrance fee here before hiking the trail. The Tejas Trail heads southwest, passing a maintenance building, and crosses a grassy meadow to a junction with Bush Mountain Trail at 0.25 mile. Go straight on Tejas Trail.

The trail follows the banks of a dry wash in twisting Upper Dog Canyon for the next 1.4 miles. Rounded limestone cobbles, swept down the creek bed by sporadic flash floods, line the rough canyon floor. A forest of scattered juniper, pine, madrone, and oak offer shade along the stony trail. Groves of bigtooth maples about a mile up the path offer garish colors in late October, usually a couple weeks before they change in McKittrick Canyon. The trail gently climbs as it heads southwest, gaining 300 feet before exiting the canyon floor.

The next 1.4-mile trail section steeply ascends the broad face of a ridge, making five looping switchbacks across barren slopes. Grass blankets the surrounding mountainsides with scattered junipers and pines growing on canyon bottoms and moister north-facing slopes. Above the switchbacks, the angle eases and the trail continues to climb the rounded ridge before making a sharp left below Lost Peak's north ridge. Tejas Trail heads south, contouring along the mountain's upper east flank. Stop at a grove of stunted trees before the trail heads across a cliff band.

Go right or west here and scramble 0.1 mile up an easy slope to the rocky summit of 7,830-foot Lost Peak, an unranked summit on a high ridge that separates Upper Dog Canyon and West Dog Canyon. This is a great spot to enjoy expansive views of the Guadalupe Mountains while eating lunch and sipping water. Continue the hike by returning east to Tejas Trail and going left, retracing your steps back to the trailhead for a 6.2-mile hike.

For extra credit, continue south on the Tejas Trail for another mile, passing through a pine forest to the junction with McKittrick Canyon Trail. Go left and hike another half-mile or so for spectacular views into rugged South McKittrick Canyon, and then follow the trails back north to the Dog Canyon Trailhead.

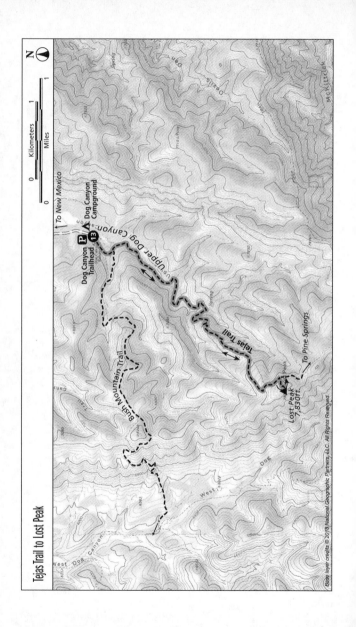

Tejas Trail to Lost Peak

Miles and Directions

0.0 Trailhead (GPS: N31 59.37' / W104 50.02')

0.25 Junction with Bush Mountain Trail (GPS: N31 59.28' / W104 50.08'). Go straight.

1.6 Leave dry wash at first switchback and begin climbing slope.

3.0 Reach trail high point and edge of trees (GPS: N31 58.14' / W104 51.13'). Go right or west up easy slope.

3.1 Hike west for 525 feet to the summit of Lost Peak (GPS: N31 58.12' / W104 51.17').

6.2 Arrive back at the trailhead.

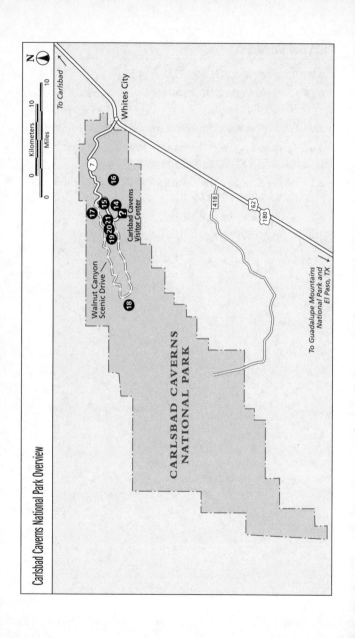

Carlsbad Caverns National Park Overview

Carlsbad Caverns National Park

Hiking in Carlsbad Caverns National Park

Carlsbad Caverns National Park, lying at the northeastern end of the Guadalupe Mountains, protects over 120 caves scattered across 46,766-acres of low limestone mountains creased by deep canyons. Most visitors head to Carlsbad Caverns, the park's most famous cave, to view its spectacular and diverse cave decorations or speleothems and numerous chambers, including the Big Room, the fifth largest chamber in the United States. The park attracts more visitors than neighboring Guadalupe Mountains National Park, with an average of 410,000 annual visitors in the ten years between 2007 and 2016.

Hikers easily explore the cavern on two self-guided tours down the Natural Entrance Trail and on the Big Room Trail, which is partially handicap-accessible, and King's Palace Trail, a ranger-led hike to protect fragile cave formations. The park also offers rugged ranger-led cave tours through Left Hand Tunnel, Hall of the White Giant, and Lower Cave in Carlsbad Caverns, and in two other caves—Spider and Slaughter Canyon caves. These tours, except King's Palace and Left Hand Tunnel, are available on a limited basis by reservation in the summer only. Check at the visitor center, park website, or recreation.gov for updated tour schedules and tickets. Besides the beautiful caves, one of the park's best attractions is the nightly bat flight between May and October when over half a million Brazilian free-tailed bats leave the cave's natural entrance around sunset.

The park's backcountry west of the visitor center and caverns is rarely visited, making it perfect for a solitary hike in the dry Chihuahuan Desert landscape. Hikers discover rounded mountains dissected by canyons, desert vegetation adapted to a harsh climate, and no flowing water.

This book describes five surface trails and three underground trails at Carlsbad Caverns National Park. While the park offers almost 50 miles of trails, most are remote and rarely used by hikers. These include Guadalupe Ridge Trail, Slaughter Canyon Trail, and Yucca Canyon Trail, which can be combined into big loops for overnight backpacking trips. These trails are not included since they require backcountry skills like route finding, and parts of the trails may have fallen into disrepair or are difficult to follow. Instead, you'll find great day hikes on kid-friendly trails, wheelchair-accessible trails, several trails that explore the backcountry, and underground trails to one of the planet's most beautiful places.

For a longer adventure, backpackers can explore the depths of Carlsbad Caverns and the highest mountain in Texas on the 100-mile-long Guadalupe Ridge Trail, a patchwork of existing trails through both national parks, Lincoln National Forest, and Bureau of Land Management public lands. The trail, opening in 2017, mostly follows the crest of the wild Guadalupe Mountains.

Finding the Park and Trailheads

Carlsbad Caverns National Park lies near New Mexico's southern border 20 miles southwest of Carlsbad, New Mexico, and 35 miles northeast of the Pine Springs Visitor

Center at Guadalupe Mountains National Park in Texas. Turn at Whites City onto NM 7 and drive 7 miles to the visitor center and cavern entrance.

Stop at the Carlsbad Caverns National Park Visitor Center to get acquainted with the park's natural history and geology, tour education exhibits, purchase tickets for entering the cave and for ranger-led tours, and to take the elevators 750 feet down to the Underground Rest Area and the trailhead for the self-guided Big Room Trail and the King's Palace Trail tour.

The trailheads for the Natural Entrance Trail, Old Guano Road Trail, and Chihuahuan Desert Nature Trail are reached by hiking 0.2 mile down a paved path from the north side of the visitor center to the Bat Flight Amphitheater. Wheelchair visitors get to the accessible section of the Chihuahuan Desert Nature Trail from a trailhead on the east side of the east parking lot at the visitor center.

The other described park trails are reached from trailheads on New Mexico 7 and on the one-way, 9.5-mile Walnut Canyon Scenic Drive, which begins west of the visitor center.

Best Seasons

Carlsbad Caverns National Park, lying in the northern Chihuahuan Desert, has a mild climate with an average of 278 sunny days a year. Mild temperatures in spring and autumn are ideal for backcountry hiking at Carlsbad Caverns, with daily highs between 65°F and 85°F. It is, however, often windy in winter and spring.

The summer months are hot, with daily highs between 90 and the low 100s. It's best to avoid hiking under the midday sun since little shade and no water is found on the trails. Plan to hike in the early morning or evening for the best temperatures. Bring plenty of water; a gallon per person per day is not too much. Sports drinks or mixes that offer electrolyte replacement are essential if you're sweating. Also, wear a hat and sunscreen for protection from the sun. Hikers have died from dehydration and sunstroke in the park, so use extreme caution in extreme temperatures. Cell phone reception is spotty in the backcountry; make sure you tell someone where you're hiking.

The bulk of the park's average 14.9 inches of precipitation falls between July and September when moist monsoon moisture pushes north, spawning thunderstorms accompanied by lightning. Winter temperatures in the 50s and 60s are perfect for hiking, with occasional snow and icy conditions. The park receives an average of 5.2 inches of snow each winter.

Camping

There are no campgrounds in the national park. The closest camping facility is an RV park at Whites City, along with motels. Otherwise look for accommodations, including private campgrounds and motels, in Carlsbad or camp at the first-come first-served Pine Springs Campground at Guadalupe Mountains National Park to the west. Free camping is available on surrounding BLM lands. Check at the Carlsbad BLM office at (575) 234-5972 for more information. Primitive camping is allowed in the park's backcountry by camping permit only. Obtain the free permit at the visitor center.

14 Chihuahuan Desert Nature Trail

A family-friendly hike that explores the desert landscape near Carlsbad Cavern's Natural Entrance and park visitor center.

Distance: 0.7 mile from east parking lot; 0.5 mile from Bat Flight Amphitheater; 0.9 mile from the visitor center
Hiking time: 30 minutes
Difficulty: Easy
Elevation gain: 60 feet
Type of hike: Lollipop; handicap-accessible hike is out and back

Best seasons: Year-round. Summer is hot.
Restrictions: No dogs allowed. Trail closed during bat flight time.
Maps: Park map; National Geographic Carlsbad Caverns National Park Trail Map 247
Trail contact: Carlsbad Caverns National Park (see appendix)

Finding the trailhead: Drive southwest from Carlsbad on US 62/180 for 20 miles to Whites City. Turn right at the signed junction on the Carlsbad Caverns Highway and drive 7 miles to the park headquarters, visitor center, and two parking lots (GPS: N32 10.30' / W104 26.39'). Start the hike and the paved handicap-accessible part of the trail at a trailhead at the east end of the east parking lot. Trailhead GPS: N32 10.31' / W104 26.29'

Alternatively, from the visitor center, follow signs for Bat Flight Amphitheater and hike 0.2 mile on a paved trail to the amphitheater. The trailhead is right of the amphitheater and before the start of the Natural Entrance Trail (GPS: N32 10.36' / W104 26.28').

The Hike

The Chihuahuan Desert Nature Trail is a partially paved, 0.7-mile lollipop hike that begins at a trailhead at the east end of the parking lot southeast of the visitor center. The paved handicap-accessible section of trail makes a 0.4-mile out-and-back hike from this trailhead. Alternatively, start the hike at the visitor center and hike to the trailhead beside the Bat Flight Amphitheater and the start of the Natural Entrance Trail; this lollipop hike is 0.9 mile round-trip from the visitor center.

The self-guided trail explores the biodiversity of the Chihuahuan Desert at Carlsbad Caverns National Park with interpretive signs that identify desert plants, animals, and native cultures. The trail can be hiked in either direction, but the signs are numbered counterclockwise along the described route.

The trail is closed in the evenings during the warmer months to avoid disturbing the flight of the Brazilian free-tailed bats exiting Carlsbad Caverns. The bats roost in the Bat Cave section of the cavern from April to October. They sleep during the day, and then escape the cave to spend the night feeding on insects. Check out this spectacular natural display from the Bat Flight Amphitheater every summer night or at dawn. The early morning flight back into the cave isn't as dramatic as the evening exit. Check at the visitor center for the estimated flight time.

Begin at the trailhead on the far eastern end of the large parking area southeast of the visitor center. Hike east for 315 feet to a junction with the return trail and the start of the loop. A left turn leads to the amphitheater and the cave's natural entrance. Go right and follow the wide trail along the crest of a ridge. Interpretive signs along the trail explain the area's natural history. Hikers learn that Native Americans made diapers from juniper bark, rope from lechuguilla, soap from Torrey yucca roots, and how catclaw acacia got its name. After 0.2 mile the trail reaches a shady ramada and views south across the west Texas plains.

The stone and wood ramada marks the end of the handicap-accessible trail, so after resting in the shade, turn around and retrace the trail 0.2 mile back to the parking area. Low stone walls just past the ramada make a narrow opening on the trail so that wheelchairs can't pass through. The trail, losing about 60 feet of elevation, begins descending here.

The trail bends north at the ramada and descends rocky slopes to a dry wash in a broad, shallow valley. Near here is a fenced second natural entrance to Carlsbad Caverns as well as two vertical shafts blasted into the Bat Cave below. Miners dug bat guano, used as a nitrate-rich fertilizer, from the cave, hauling it 170 feet up the shafts in buckets. The valuable guano was taken down a rough road, now the Old Guano Road Trail, to Whites City and then shipped to California for the growing citrus industry. Starting in 1903, an estimated 100,000 tons of guano, about 90 percent of the cave's deposit, was removed over twenty years from the cave.

The junction with Old Guano Road Trail is reached after 0.4 mile. Go left or west on the dirt trail, passing more interpretive signs. The trail and cavern area lies in the northern Chihuahuan Desert, which stretches south into Mexico. The barren land is characterized by desert plants, including creosote bush, mesquite, prickly pear, sotol yucca, and lechuguilla, an agave that is an indicator plant for the Chihuahuan Desert. Seldom-seen wildlife includes mule deer, coyote, foxes, rabbits, and ringtails, along with over three hundred bird species in the national park. Rattlesnakes are present, but rarely seen.

After 0.55 mile the trail reaches a junction on the south side of the Bat Flight Amphitheater and at the trailhead for the Natural Entrance Trail. Go left on a paved trail and reach another junction in a couple hundred feet. Go left to another

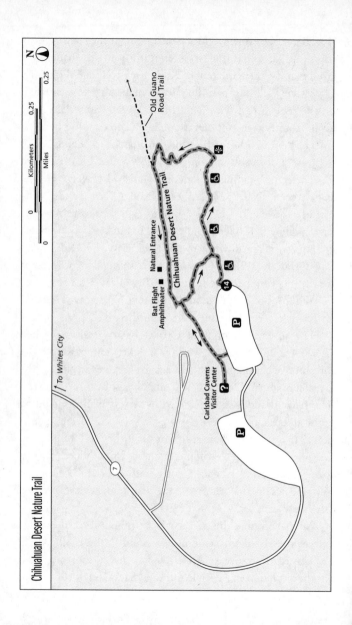

Chihuahuan Desert Nature Trail

To Whites City

Bat Flight Amphitheater

Natural Entrance

Old Guano Road Trail

Chihuahuan Desert Nature Trail

Carlsbad Caverns Visitor Center

P

P

7

14

N

0   0.25
Kilometers

0   0.25
Miles

junction. A right turn heads 0.12 mile southwest on a paved trail to the visitor center. To complete the hike, go left and hike up a gradual hill on the paved trail to the final junction. Take a right and hike west to the trailhead and parking lot.

Miles and Directions

0.0   Trailhead at east end of parking area (GPS: N32 10.31' / W104 26.29').

0.1   Junction with loop trail. Go right.

0.2   Shade ramada with bench. End of handicap-accessible trail.

0.4   Junction with Old Guano Road Trail (GPS: N32 10.37' / W104 26.18'). Go left or west on dirt trail.

0.5   Junction with Natural Entrance Trailhead at Bat Flight Amphitheater (GPS: N32 10.36' / W104 26.28'). Go left on paved trail.

0.62 Junction. Go left on paved trail.

0.63 Junction with paved trail from visitor center. Keep left on hike or go right to visitor center.

0.68 Junction at end of loop. Go right 300 feet to trailhead and parking area.

0.7   Arrive back at the trailhead.

15 Walnut Canyon Vista Trail

A short paved trail through scrubby desert terrain to an over-look above Walnut Canyon.

Distance: 0.1 mile or 540 feet
Hiking time: 30 minutes
Difficulty: Easy
Elevation gain: 10 feet
Type of hike: Out-and-back
Best seasons: Year-round. Summer days are hot.

Restrictions: Open year-round with no restrictions. No dogs or pets allowed.
Maps: Park map; National Geographic Carlsbad Caverns National Park Trail Map 247
Trail contact: Carlsbad Caverns National Park (see appendix)

Finding the trailhead: Drive southwest from Carlsbad on US 62/180 for 20 miles to Whites City. Turn right at the signed junction on the Carlsbad Caverns Highway and drive 5.8 miles to a pullover on the right or north side of the road. Trailhead GPS: N32 10.55' / W104 26.02'

The Hike

The Walnut Canyon Vista Trail is a short hike through a typical Chihuahuan desert ecosystem to a viewpoint above Walnut Canyon, a twisting canyon that drains southeast to Whites City. Walnut Canyon is floored by a dry wash filled with rounded limestone boulders and cobbles. Small walnut trees scatter along the wash, giving the canyon its name. The Carlsbad Caverns Highway follows the canyon floor before climbing up a steep grade, locally called the Big Hill, below the trail's overlook to a rounded plateau and the cavern.

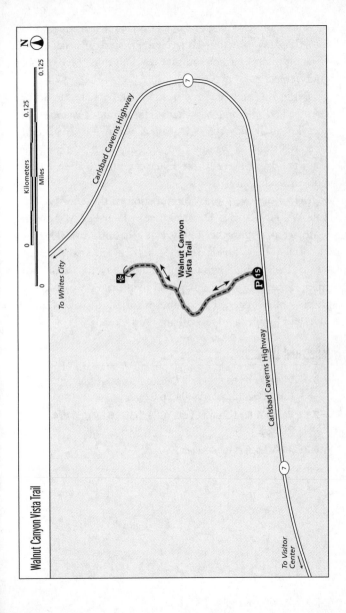

Walnut Canyon Vista Trail

Carlsbad Caverns Highway

Walnut Canyon
Vista Trail

P 15

Carlsbad Caverns Highway

To Whites City

To Visitor
Center

7

7

N

Kilometers
0   0.125

Miles
0   0.125

The short trail is easy to follow and offers great views into the canyon below. Bring water and wear a hat if you walk the trail on a hot summer day, and don't leave pets in your vehicle.

Begin the hike at a trailhead at a long pullover on the north side of the highway after it climbs out of Walnut Canyon. The trail dips across a shallow wash, and then gently ascends a slope to Walnut Canyon Vista on top of a broken limestone layer. Reverse the hike to return to the trailhead and your vehicle.

Below the overlook is the junction of the one-way, 9.5-mile Walnut Canyon Desert Drive, which begins near the visitor center, with the highway at a hairpin turn. The scenic drive follows a ridge to the rim of Rattlesnake Canyon before descending down upper Walnut Canyon to a junction. After visiting the cave, this gravel road makes a worthwhile afternoon excursion. The trailheads for Rattlesnake Canyon Trail and Juniper Ridge Trail are on the road.

Miles and Directions

0.0 Trailhead on north side of Carlsbad Caverns Highway (GPS: N32 10.55' / W104 26.02').

0.1 Reach Walnut Canyon Vista (GPS: N32 10.59' / W104 26.02').

0.2 Arrive back at the trailhead.

16 Old Guano Road Trail

An easy hike from Carlsbad Cavern's Natural Entrance down a long ridge to Whites City.

Distance: 3.7 miles one-way if using a car shuttle; 7.4 miles round-trip

Hiking time: 2 hours one-way

Difficulty: Moderately easy

Elevation gain: 710-foot loss from Natural Entrance to Whites City

Type of hike: Out-and-back or car shuttle

Best seasons: Autumn, winter, and spring. Summer days are hot and no shade is along the trail.

Restrictions: No dogs

Maps: Park map; National Geographic Carlsbad Caverns National Park Trail Map 247

Trail contact: Carlsbad Caverns National Park (see appendix)

Finding the trailhead: Drive southwest from Carlsbad on US 62/180 for 20 miles to Whites City. Turn right at the signed junction on the Carlsbad Caverns Highway and drive 7 miles to the park headquarters, visitor center, and two parking lots. Trailhead GPS: N32 10.30' / W104 26.39'

From the visitor center, hike northeast for 0.2 mile on a paved trail to the amphitheater, following signs for Bat Flight Amphitheater. The trailhead is right of the amphitheater and before the start of the Natural Entrance Trail. Trailhead GPS: N32 10.36' / W104 26.28'

The Hike

The Old Guano Road Trail descends 710 feet in 3.7 miles from the Natural Entrance of Carlsbad Caverns to a trailhead on the west side of a private campground in Whites City. The easy trail, following an historic roadway, is best hiked from the west trailhead by the visitor center since it gently descends a broad ridge to the east trailhead. The difficulty in hiking it one-way is that you need to get back to your vehicle at the visitor center. It's best to arrange a shuttle pick-up at Whites City with one of your party. Alternatively, do it as an out-and-back hike by following the trail until you feel like turning around and returning to the visitor center.

The trail, an old doubletrack wagon road, is best hiked in the cooler months. Summer hiking, except in the early morning or late afternoon, is discouraged since the trail is sunny and hot, with no shade along the track. Be prepared for desert hiking by carrying plenty of water and wearing a hat and sunscreen. Also pay attention to the weather, the open ridge is dangerous in a lightning storm. Most of the trail is easy to follow, with cairns and park markers indicating the route when it passes over rocky sections.

Start the hike at the east side of the park visitor center. Follow a 0.2-mile-long paved trail to the Bat Flight Amphitheater by the cavern's Natural Entrance. The trailhead for the Old Guano Road Trail and the Chihuahuan Desert Nature Trail is on the right side of the amphitheater.

Go right on the dirt trail and hike east 0.17 mile to a junction. This trail section is shared with the Chihuahuan Desert Nature Trail, which goes right at the junction. The nature trail offers interpretive signs explaining plants of the upper Chihuahuan Desert. Continue straight and after a quarter mile, you reach a second cave entrance and nearby shaft that was blasted into the Bat Cave below. A fence surrounds the entrance. A second shaft was dug about 1/8-mile to the east.

After the discovery of Carlsbad Caverns in the late 1800s, enterprising locals began excavating guano, a nitrogen-rich fertilizer deposited by millions of bats. Abijah Long filed a

Old Guano Road Trail

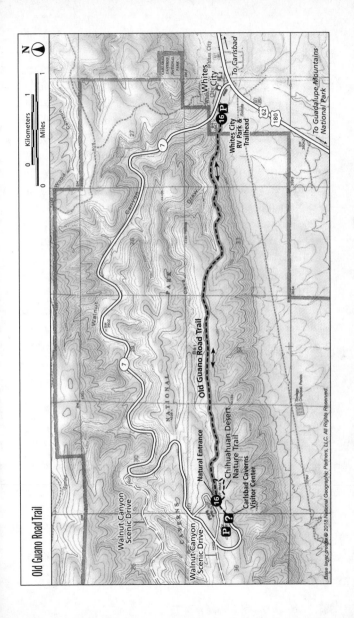

40-acre claim in 1903 to mine the guano and other minerals at the cave mouth. Two vertical shafts were later dug to easily haul the guano to the surface, where it was loaded in wagons and hauled down the Guano Road to Whites City. It was then shipped by rail to California to fertilize citrus groves. Over 100,000 tons of guano was mined from the cave before operations ceased in the 1920s. Before trails were made into the cave, visitors were lowered two at a time in ore buckets down the shafts to the cave floor 170 feet below.

The trail passes the right side of the fence and continues east. Near the fenced area are scattered tin cans, lids, bits of glass, and pottery shards left by visitors in the early 1900s. These are part of the historic record, so leave them in place for other hikers to enjoy.

The trail narrows as it begins to descend toward Whites City. Views spread out below the high ridge. Canyons, lined with cliff bands, stretch to the north while the arid Texas plains lie to the south and the Guadalupe Mountains to the west. After 2.7 miles the trail begins to descend a steep section, with Whites City below. Pay attention since the trail passes over bedrock and can be lost. At the bottom of the ridge the trail passes through a fence that marks the park boundary and enters a private campground on the west side of Whites City.

Return up the trail for a 7.4-mile round-trip hike or catch a ride back to your vehicle at the visitor center.

Miles and Directions

- **0.0** Trailhead at Bat Flight Amphitheater and trailhead for Natural Entrance Trail (GPS: N32 10.36' / W104 26.28').
- **0.17** Reach a junction with Chihuahuan Desert Nature Trail (GPS: N32 10.37' / W104 26.18'). Go straight.

0.25 Reach a fenced cave entrance and shaft. Go right around fence.

2.7 Begin steeper descent.

3.7 Trail's end at private campground (GPS: N32 10.33' / W104 22.58'). Hike back to visitor center parking lot or catch a ride.

17 Juniper Ridge Trail

A moderate out-and-back hike up gentle, rocky slopes to a high ridgeline on the national park's northern boundary.

Distance: 1.8 miles round-trip
Hiking time: 1-2 hours
Difficulty: Moderate
Elevation gain: 450 feet
Type of hike: Out-and-back
Best seasons: Autumn, winter, and spring. Summer is hot.

Restrictions: No dogs allowed
Maps: Park map; National Geographic Carlsbad Caverns National Park Trail Map 247
Trail contact: Carlsbad Caverns National Park (see appendix)

Finding the trailhead: From Whites City and US 62/180, drive the Carlsbad Caverns Highway (County Road 7) for 6.5 miles and turn right or west on Walnut Canyon Scenic Drive. This junction is a half-mile before the park visitor center. Follow the gravel, 9.5-mile road for 8.9 miles to a pull off on the right side of the road. Cross the road to the trailhead, marked by a small sign. Trailhead GPS: N32 11.10' / W104 26.42'

The Hike

The Juniper Ridge Trail is a 0.9-mile singletrack trail up gentle slopes to the northern boundary fence of Carlsbad Caverns National Park on top of broad Juniper Ridge. The 1.8-mile round-trip hike, gaining 500 feet of elevation from the trailhead on Walnut Canyon Scenic Drive to the fence line, offers easy hiking and gentle grades through a typical Chihuahuan Desert ecosystem. The hike makes a great introduction to desert hiking, with wildlife, an easy-to-follow trail, and spacious views across the eastern Guadalupe Mountains.

The trail crosses open terrain so it can be windy and is hot in summer. Get an early start during the warmer months and bring water or sports drinks, a hat, and sunscreen. It's best to avoid this hike during the blazing hot of a summer day. The trail is lightly used so vegetation, including cacti and yucca, lines the path. Most of the trail is well defined but several sections cross rocky terrain so keep watch for cairns of stacked white boulders to mark the way. Don't build extra cairns here or on other park trails since they're unnecessary and damage the desert ecosystem.

Begin the hike at a trailhead on the north side of the gravel Walnut Canyon Scenic Drive opposite a parking area. The trail heads northwest through short grass and scrub, and then climbs past a couple broken rock bands onto a terrace above the second rock band and a shallow canyon. Hike north along the terrace, before cutting left and scrambling over bedrock on a wide ridge. Higher the trail curves around the head of another canyon lined with short cliffs and filled with trees, a sure sign of water. After 0.9 mile, the trail reaches the broad top of Juniper Ridge and a barbed wire fence that marks the park boundary.

This place, the turn-around spot for the hike, is a good place to stop for a drink of water and to enjoy the view. The higher mountains in neighboring Guadalupe Mountains National Park rise above rounded ridges and shallow canyons to the southwest. The park visitor center sits on the mesa top on the opposite side of Walnut Canyon to the south, while low ridges and hills spread to the northern horizon. Return down the trail to the scenic drive for a 1.9-mile hike.

You can stretch the hike out from the end point by continuing west on the trail along the fence for another half-mile or so before it peters out. The trail is usually marked with

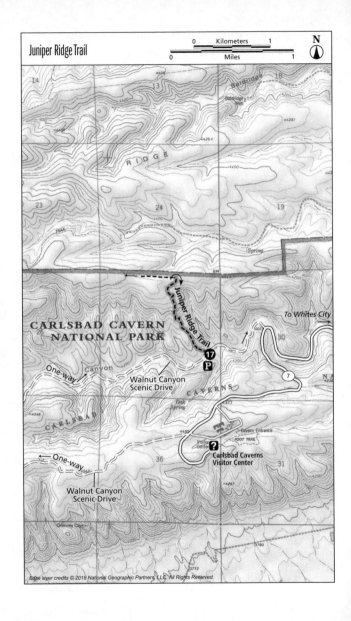

Juniper Ridge Trail

0   Kilometers   1

0   Miles   1

N

Bettridge
Bettridge's
Well

RIDGE

Spring

Juniper Ridge Trail

BM

To Whites City

CARLSBAD CAVERN
NATIONAL PARK

17
P

One-way   Canyon

Walnut Canyon
Scenic Drive

CAVERNS

Oak
Spring

Cavern Entrance
FOOT TRAIL

Visitor
Center

?

Carlsbad Caverns
Visitor Center

One-way

Walnut Canyon
Scenic Drive

Chimney Cave

cairns. If you do this extension, be sure to remember where the trail meets the fence line so you take the correct fork to get back to the trailhead. It's easy to miss the turn since cairns mark another trail extension that heads east along the fence.

Be alert when hiking the trail for rattlesnakes in nearby rocks as well as other animals, especially at the small riparian zone in the canyon near the top of the hike. Large mammals include coyote, deer, pronghorn, javelina, mountain lion, and Barbary sheep, an introduced African species. The best time to spot animals and birds is in the early morning.

Miles and Directions

0.0 Trailhead on Walnut Canyon Desert Drive (GPS: N32 11.10' / W104 26.42').

0.9 Reach national park boundary and turn-around point (GPS: N32 11.40' / W104 26.59').

1.8 Arrive back at the trailhead.

18 Rattlesnake Canyon Trail

Two out-and-back hikes of different difficulties to a view-point above Rattlesnake Canyon and to the wash in Rattle-snake Canyon in the remote western part of the national park.

Distance: 0.8 mile round-trip for short hike; 1.8 miles round-trip to Rattlesnake Canyon
Hiking time: 1–3 hours
Difficulty: Easy and moderate
Elevation gain: 200-foot loss and gain
Type of hike: Out-and-back trail
Best seasons: Year-round. Oct through Apr is best. Summers are hot.

Restrictions: Dogs not allowed. No fires. Backcountry permit required for camping.
Maps: USGS Quad; National Geographic Carlsbad Caverns National Park Trail Map 247; park map
Trail contact: Carlsbad Caverns National Park (see appendix)

Finding the trailhead: From Whites City and US 62/180, drive the Carlsbad Caverns Highway (County Road 7) for 6.5 miles and turn right or west on Walnut Canyon Scenic Drive. This junction is a half-mile before the park visitor center. Follow the gravel, 9.5-mile road for 3.7 miles to a two-car parking area on the left side of the road at interpretive marker #9 and the Rattlesnake Canyon Trailhead. Trailhead GPS: N32 09.56' / W104 30.11'

The Hike

Rattlesnake Canyon Trail, a moderately strenuous 6-mile out-and-back hike, is easily shortened to a 0.9-mile round-trip hike to a scenic viewpoint or a 1.9-mile round-trip trek to the floor of Rattlesnake Canyon where North and South Rattlesnake Canyons meet. The short hike makes an easy hour-long excursion that's perfect for families or hikers wanting a quick fix. The longer hike to the bottom of the canyon is more difficult, losing 500 feet of elevation, which has to be regained back to the trailhead above. Only skilled desert hikers will want to do the longer six-mile, round-trip hike down Rattlesnake Canyon to Carlsbad Cavern's southern boundary and back since the rugged trail crosses a stony wash many times.

It's best to hike the singletrack trail in the cooler months between October and April. Summer days are usually hot and sunny, with almost no shade along the trail and the hike back out of Rattlesnake Canyon is steep. If you plan hiking in summer, get an early morning start for cool temperatures. Be prepared for desert hiking by carrying plenty of water, a gallon per person in summer is not too much, and wearing sunscreen and a hat. Rattlesnake Canyon Trail is easy to follow from the trailhead to the canyon floor, with occasional cairns making the path when it crosses rocky sections.

Start the hike by driving 3.7 miles west on the one-way Walnut Canyon Scenic Drive, which begins a half-mile before the park visitor center. The marked trailhead at 4,517 feet is on the left side of the narrow dirt road on a high ridge. The trail descends a rocky slope and reaches the bottom of a shallow canyon after 450 feet. The trail follows the canyon floor and after 0.15 mile it begins traversing across a narrow bench below a broken cliff band. The unnamed canyon drops away below the trail.

The trail spirals around the mountainside, gently descending to boulders above the deepening canyon. This point, 0.4 mile from the trailhead, is the turn-around spot if you want an easy hike. Stop at the boulders and enjoy the view into Rattlesnake Canyon with its white wash gleaming in the sunlight. High ridges lift rounded shoulders above the canyon, their steep flanks creased by horizontal bands of limestone. Return to the trailhead from here for a short 0.8-mile hike.

If you're energetic, follow the trail down from the boulders. It steeply descends 200 feet in 0.15 mile on a half-dozen switchbacks over loose, rocky terrain to the bottom of the side canyon at 4,200 feet. Continue along the north side of the rough canyon floor for another 0.3 mile to the wide wash on the floor of Rattlesnake Canyon. This turn-around point is 0.9 mile from the trailhead. The two branches of the canyon, North Rattlesnake Canyon and South Rattlesnake Canyon, meet a hundred feet up the canyon. The deep sinuous canyons begin on a high ridge to the west that separates them from Slaughter Canyon. To complete the hike, head back up the path and reach the trailhead for a 1.8-mile round-trip hike.

If you want to explore more of Rattlesnake Canyon, head down the rough trail along the canyon floor. It crosses the stony wash many times and sometimes fades away in brush. Look for occasional cairns to keep on track. After a half-mile or 1.7 miles from the trailhead, the trail passes the old concrete foundation of the historic Stone Ranch, which operated here in the early twentieth century. The ranch obtained water from Stone Spring high in cliffs on the west side of the canyon.

This area of the national park is remote, quiet, and filled with wildlife. Keep alert for mule deer, Barbary sheep, and, of course, rattlesnakes. The trail continues south along the canyon floor for another mile or so to the mouth of Rattlesnake Canyon. Turn around wherever you want and retrace your steps back to the trailhead for a full day of hiking. The area south of the Carlsbad Caverns National Park boundary is private property.

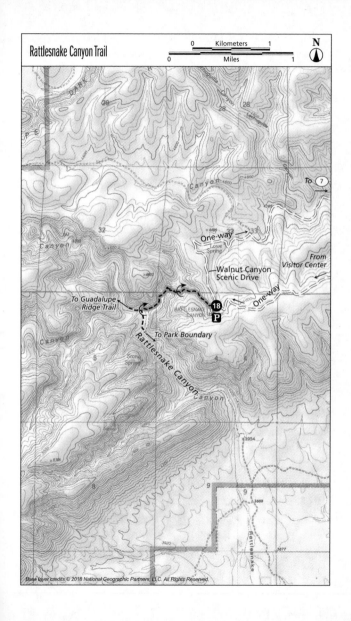

Rattlesnake Canyon Trail

Rattlesnake Canyon Trail offers great camping, especially on the grassy benches in the main canyon. Backcountry camping is allowed west of the Rattlesnake Canyon Trailhead and south of Guadalupe Ridge Trail on the north side of the national park. Camp at least 100 feet from established trails, 300 feet from water sources, and a half-mile from the scenic road. Obtain a required free backcountry camping permit from the visitor center before heading out.

Miles and Directions

0.0 Rattlesnake Canyon Trailhead on the Walnut Canyon Scenic Drive (GPS: N32 09.56' / W104 30.11').

450 ft Reach the bottom of the canyon.

0.15 Trail leaves the canyon floor and begins traversing across mountainside.

0.4 Turn-around point above switchbacks for short, easy hike (GPS: N32 10.01' / W104 30.32').

0.8 Arrive back at the trailhead.

Round-trip to bottom of Rattlesnake Canyon

0.0 Rattlesnake Canyon Trailhead on the Walnut Canyon Scenic Drive (GPS: N32 09.56' / W104 30.11').

450 ft Reach the bottom of the canyon.

0.15 Trail leaves the canyon floor and begins traversing across mountainside.

0.4 Turn-around point above switchbacks for short, easy hike (GPS: N32 10.01' / W104 30.32').

0.55 Reach the bottom of the canyon, descending 200 feet.

0.9 Bottom of wide wash in Rattlesnake Canyon (GPS: N32 09.54' / W104 30.49').

1.8 Arrive back at the trailhead.

Cave Trails

19 Natural Entrance Trail

The scenic trail descends 750 feet from the Natural Entrance, used by bats, to elevators that return you to the surface. The paved trail passes numerous cave features, including Devil's Spring, Witch's Fingers, Iceberg Rock, and The Boneyard.

Distance: 1.25 miles one-way from cave entrance to elevators; 2.5-mile out-and-back hike

Hiking time: 1 hour for descent; 1-2 hours for ascent

Difficulty: Moderate—not recommended for visitors with heart, breathing, or walking difficulties

Elevation gain: 750-foot descent. Ride elevator or hike trail back to surface for 750-foot gain.

Type of hike: One-way or out-and-back

Best seasons: Year-round. The underground temperature remains at 56°F.

Restrictions: Anyone under age sixteen must be accompanied by an adult. No strollers, pets, or tobacco products. Stay on the trail at all times. No food or drink except bottled water.

Schedule: Check at the visitor center for updated times. Summer (Memorial Day through Labor Day weekends): Trail opens at 8:30 a.m.; last elevator out at 6:30 p.m. Last time to hike trail is 4 p.m. Last time to hike out trail is 4 p.m.; must reach surface by 5 p.m. Fall/Winter/Spring (Labor Day through Memorial Day weekends): Trail opens at 8:30 a.m., last elevator out at 4:30 p.m. Last time to hike out trail is 2 p.m.; must reach surface by 3 p.m.

Maps: Park map; National Geographic Carlsbad Caverns National Park Trail Map 247

Trail contact: Carlsbad Caverns National Park (see appendix)

Finding the trailhead: Drive southwest from Carlsbad on US 62/ 180 for 20 miles to Whites City. Turn right at the signed junction on the Carlsbad Caverns Highway and drive 7 miles to the park head-quarters, visitor center, and two parking lots (GPS: N32 10.30' / W104

26.39'). From the east parking lot and the east side of the visitor center, follow signs for Bat Flight Amphitheater and hike 0.2 mile on a paved trail to the start of the Natural Entrance Trail by the amphitheater. Trailhead GPS: N32 10.30' / W104 26.39'

The Hike

The Natural Entrance Trail, a 1.25-mile self-guided trail, descends over 750 feet from Carlsbad Caverns' wide natural entrance to two elevators that whisk you back to the surface inside the visitor center. This self-guided trail is a great introduction to the cave and, when combined with a 1.2-mile hike through the Big Room, is the best way to see all of the notable and popular cave features. Interpretive signs along the paved trail explain the story of Carlsbad Caverns. Visitors can also rent an informative audio guide at the bookstore that explains the cavern at numbered stops along the trail.

Hikers should be healthy, physically fit, and without heart, breathing, or walking difficulties. Your cell phone won't work in the cave, so telephones are scattered along the trail for emergency use. The park recommends turning off your phone or putting it on airplane mode so its battery doesn't drain while searching for a signal while underground. Wear sturdy shoes or boots. Eat and drink before entering the cave on the trail since you aren't allowed to bring food or drinks, other than bottled water, into the cave. The inside temperature of the cave remains at a steady 56°F year-round, despite hot summer temperatures on the surface. Pack an extra layer of warm clothes like a sweatshirt or light coat. Also bring a flashlight and extra batteries to illuminate cave features and your camera. Flash photography and tripods are allowed but be mindful of other visitors. Lastly, use a quiet voice since sound travels as much as a quarter mile in the cave.

Begin the hike at the east side of the park visitor center. Follow a 0.2-mile-long paved trail to the Bat Flight Amphitheater above the cavern's Natural Entrance. Here you show your cave tickets (good for three days) and listen to a ranger-led safety talk. The paved trail, lined with low stone walls, switchbacks down into the gaping mouth of the cave. Overhanging limestone cliffs tower above the trail, and cliff swallows swoop through the air catching insects during warm months. The first trail section, with eighteen switchbacks, steeply descends 200 feet down the sloped entrance corridor.

The natural entrance formed between two and three million years ago when a section of limestone collapsed, opening the dark rooms and passageways to the outside world. This allowed Carlsbad Caverns to become a breathing cave with air circulation. While Native Americans descended into the upper cave, nineteenth-century cowboys later found the cave by investigating "smoke" coming from the ground. The smoke turned out to be bats leaving the cave in the early evening.

The bats roost in the Bat Cave room below the natural entrance. This area is closed to public access, so you won't see the bats. Mexican free-tailed bats, also called Brazilian free-tailed bats, roost in the cave from April to October, sleeping in the cave during daylight hours and then making a mass exodus at dusk to spend the night feasting on insects. You can witness this fascinating display from the Bat Flight Amphitheater at the cave entrance every summer night. Check at the visitor center for the current flight time. Fringed and Cave Myotis bats also roost in the deepest part of the cave at Lake of the Clouds, which is not open to the public.

The trail enters the twilight zone, receiving faint light from the surface, as it descends to the Bat Cave. Here the trail bends right and begins a long descent down the Main Corridor. Numerous speleothems or cave formations like stalactites, stalagmites, flowstone, and other formations line the trail. Devil's Spring, the first decorated area, is a standing pool of water with a column and other features. Beyond the spring, the trail descends steeply down fourteen switchbacks and loses another 300 feet of elevation to a pit called Devil's Den. The path is lined with a low stone wall and hand railing.

Continuing down the huge passage, the trail passes through open areas, twists down rocky slopes, and ducks under fallen boulders. Two of the best are the Witch's Fingers, tall, crooked stalagmites towering over the trail. The thin stalagmites were formed by slow drips of water over a long period of time. Iceberg Rock, a gigantic 200,000-ton boulder, sits beside the trail below several switchbacks. Like an iceberg, only the upper tip of the 170-foot-long boulder is visible from the trail. The rock fell from the ceiling between 200,000 and 500,000 years ago.

Below Iceberg Rock, the trail offers a view of Green Lake Room from an overlook. Green Lake is a cave pool fed by constant dripping water. Beyond it is the King's Palace, Queen's Chamber, and Papoose Room, which can be visited only on a ranger-led tour. The trail continues down Appetite Hill, passing beneath the bottom of Iceberg Rock, to The Boneyard. The limestone here is pocked with holes like Swiss cheese that were formed by acidic groundwater, which filtered down through thin cracks.

The trail bends left and reaches a cave map and signs at the entrance to the Big Room Trail. Turn left to the restrooms (waste water is pumped to the surface), lunch room, and rest area. You can take an elevator back to the surface

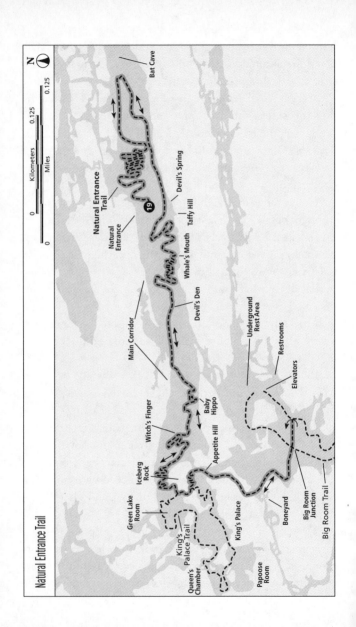

Natural Entrance Trail

750 feet above, but you'll miss the best part of the accessible cavern—the Big Room. Explore the room on the 1.25-mile, self-guided loop Big Room Trail.

Miles and Directions

0.0 Start of trail at Bat Flight Amphitheater on surface.

1.2 Reach the Big Room Junction. Go left to the rest area, lunch room, restrooms, and elevators. Go straight to hike the Big Room Trail.

20 Big Room Trail

An easy loop hike on a paved trail that explores the decorated Big Room, the fifth largest underground chamber in the United States.

Distance: 1.25 miles
Hiking time: 1–2 hours
Difficulty: Easy
Elevation gain: Less than 50 feet
Type of hike: Paved loop trail.
Best seasons: Year-round. The underground temperature remains at about 56°F.
Restrictions: Anyone under age sixteen must be accompanied by an adult. No strollers, pets, or tobacco products. Stay on the trail at all times. No food or drink except bottled water.
Schedule: Check at the visitor center for updated times.

Memorial Day through Labor Day weekends: 8:30 a.m. to 6:30 p.m. Last elevator into cave is 5 p.m.; last elevator out is 6:30 p.m. Labor Day through Memorial Day weekends: 8:30 a.m. to 4:30 p.m. Last elevator into cave is 3:30 p.m.; last elevator out is 4:30 p.m.
Maps: Park map; National Geographic Carlsbad Caverns National Park Trail Map 247
Trail contact: Carlsbad Caverns National Park (see appendix)

Finding the trailhead: Drive southwest from Carlsbad on US 62/180 for 20 miles to Whites City. Turn right at the signed junction on the Carlsbad Caverns Highway and drive 7 miles to the park headquarters, visitor center, and two parking lots. Reach the underground trailhead by taking an elevator down from the visitor center or by hiking down the Natural Entrance Trail. Trailhead GPS: N32 10.30' / W104 26.39'

The Hike

The Big Room Trail, a 1.25-mile self-guided trail, is the best and most popular way to discover the subterranean wonders of Carlsbad Caverns, the fifth largest cave in the United States. The trailhead is at the underground rest area, which is easily reached by taking an elevator down 750 feet from the park visitor center on the surface. The trailhead can also be accessed by descending the 1.2-mile Natural Entrance Trail.

The trail makes a loop around the perimeter of the Big Room. A shortcut partway along the trail allows for an abbreviated 0.75-mile hike for those who don't want to walk the entire trail. The paved trail is mostly level, with a few short hills, and is well lighted. Safety hand rails line most of the trail. Part of the trail is wheelchair accessible, but strollers are never allowed. Interpretive signs, in both English and Spanish, along the trail explain the geology and history of Carlsbad Caverns. An audio guide, available for a fee from the visitor center's bookstore, explains the room at numbered stops.

The easy trail is accessible for most visitors, including those with walking difficulties or wheelchairs. Your cell phone doesn't work in the cave, so telephones are scattered along the trail for emergency use. The park recommends turning off your phone or putting it on airplane mode. Sturdy shoes or boots with a non-skid sole are recommended. Eat and drink before entering the cave since you aren't allowed to bring food or drinks, other than plain bottled water, into the cave.

The inside temperature of the cave remains about 56°F year-round. Pack an extra layer of clothes like a sweatshirt or light coat. Also, bring a flashlight and extra batteries to illuminate cave features as well as your camera. Flash photography and tripods are allowed but photographers should be mindful of other visitors. Serious photographers should plan on visiting early in the morning or on days when the cave isn't busy. Lastly, use a quiet voice since sound travels as much as a quarter mile in the cave.

About two-thirds of the Big Room Trail is accessible to wheelchair visitors with assistance. The paved trail has a non-skid surface but is rough and uneven. An access guide, available at the visitor center information desk, has a map that shows which parts of the trail are open to wheelchairs and which are closed because of steep grades and a narrow trail. Barriers keep wheelchairs from entering closed trail sections. About half of the 1.25-mile Big Room Trail or 0.64 mile is open to wheelchairs; the round-trip hike for wheelchair users who go out to each barrier and then return to the trailhead is 1.26 miles. Rest benches are found along the trail. Accessible restrooms are in the Underground Rest Area.

Start the Big Room Trail by either descending the elevators or hiking down the Natural Entrance Trail. From the Underground Rest Area by the elevators, follow the trail in front of the lunchroom through a couple rooms to the marked Big Room Junction at the end of the Natural Entrance Trail. A sign here points the way to the Big Room and the return trail to the rest area and has a trail map. Go left on the Big Room Trail.

The Big Room, the largest chamber in Carlsbad Caverns and the fifth largest in North America, is an immense underground opening that covers over 600,000 square feet or the area of about fourteen football fields. The room is highly decorated with various speleothems, including stalactites, stalagmites, draperies, columns, soda straws, popcorn, and others. These form over hundreds of thousands of years when calcium bicarbonate solution in ground water seeps into the cave through thin fissures in the limestone above the Big Room. As the solution is exposed to air, carbon dioxide gas is released, leaving calcite behind, which slowly grows into the cave features.

The first trail section edges along the right wall of the room, passing named features like the Sword of Damocles, a stalactite that looks like a sword, and the Lion's Trail, a hanging stalactite with a bulbous end covered with cave popcorn. The spectacular Hall of Giants has some of the cave's largest features, including the Twin Domes, two massive stalagmites that tower 58 feet above the trail, and Giant Dome, a 62-foot column that is a stalagmite joined to a smaller stalactite. These formations were formed by drops of calcite-laden water that dripped from the ceiling onto the cave floor. Other named features on this section include small popcorn-covered stalagmites on the floor of Fairyland, a tall column called the Temple of the Sun, and the Breast of Venus.

After almost a third of a mile, the trail reaches a major junction. A left turn is a shortcut across the room to the return trail, which leads a half-mile to the elevators for a 0.75-mile hike. It's also where wheelchair visitors can go left to visit Crystal Spring Dome and Bottomless Pit. Keep right on the main trail to visit the largest section of the Big Room. It is one mile from here back to the elevators.

The trail passes the Cave Man, a bulky stalagmite that resembles a thinking caveman on a flowstone pedestal, and reaches the Totem Pole. This tall spindly stalagmite was formed by the constant drip of a single drop over tens of thousands of years. The ceiling above is a hanging forest of stalactites and an illuminated drapery called The Chandelier. The trail continues past a hole with a decrepit wire ladder that descends 90 feet down to the Lower Cave, another level below the Big Room. Jim White, an early cave explorer, built the ladder in 1924 for a National Geographic Society expedition.

The next stop is an overlook called the Jumping Off Place above the Lower Cave, an undeveloped section with a mile of passages. Wheelchairs must turn around here since the trail narrows and heads up a hill before descending to a left turn that leads to a seating area and viewpoint at the Top of the Cross. The end section of the Big Room has a shape roughly like an inverted giant cross, with the arms extending out to both sides and the high main corridor reaching back to the Hall of the Giants.

The trail heads along the back wall of the Big Room, passing a pool called Mirror Lake. Note that the sign marking the feature has reversed lettering so you read it in reflection when water droplets aren't dripping into the pool. The Bottomless Pit is a deep, dark abyss. Early cave explorers like Jim White only had faint lanterns to illuminate features so the gaping pit appeared bottomless in the dark. The bottom of the hole is 140 feet below the trail. Above the pit rises Liberty Dome, an immense cavity formed by acid that eroded the limestone when water filled the cavern. The distance from the top of the dome to the bottom of the pit is 370 feet, the greatest vertical distance in the cave.

The trail crosses boulders and debris that fell from the high ceiling along the wall of the cave and passes a gypsum deposit. Farther along it reaches a junction with the shortcut trail and a dramatic panorama of cave decorations, including the Totem Pole, Cave Man, and The Chandelier. Crystal

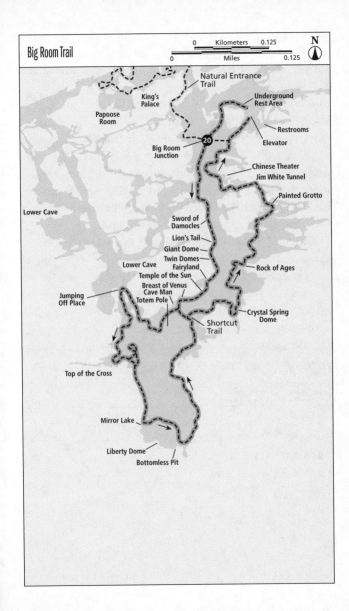

Big Room Trail

0   Kilometers   0.125
0   Miles   0.125

N

Natural Entrance Trail

King's Palace

Papoose Room

Underground Rest Area

Restrooms

Elevator

20
Big Room Junction

Chinese Theater
Jim White Tunnel

Painted Grotto

Lower Cave

Sword of Damocles

Lion's Tail

Giant Dome

Twin Domes

Fairyland

Lower Cave

Temple of the Sun

Rock of Ages

Breast of Venus
Cave Man

Totem Pole

Jumping Off Place

Crystal Spring Dome

Shortcut Trail

Top of the Cross

Mirror Lake

Liberty Dome

Bottomless Pit

Spring Dome, sitting on a sharp bend, is a glittering stalagmite that is one of many active formations in the cave. Water drips from the ceiling onto the formation and collects in a pool at its base.

Continue down the corridor with views of the Hall of Giants, and then climb a short hill to the Rock of Ages, a towering stalagmite beside the trail. After the Giants, the trail enters a smaller corridor and passes the Paintbrush, Painted Grotto, and the exquisite Doll's Theater, a small antechamber filled with thin stalactites and columns. The trail enters Jim White Tunnel to the Chinese Theater, with delicate formations shaped like a Chinese dancer or pagoda.

The trail ends at a junction 100 feet from the Natural Entrance Trail and Big Room Trail junction. Go right to the elevators and the Underground Rest Area where you can purchase basic food items as well as a postcard stamped "Mailed from 750 feet below ground." Take the elevator 750 feet back to the visitor center. Be prepared to wait in line if the cave is busy, particularly on summer and holiday weekends, or hike up the Natural Entrance Trail to the surface.

Miles and Directions

0.0 Start at the junction of the Natural Entrance Trail and the Big Room Trail near the elevators.

0.25 Junction with Shortcut Trail. Go straight.

0.55 Bottomless Pit.

0.85 Crystal Spring Dome.

1.25 Arrive back at the trailhead.

21 King's Palace Trail

A ranger-led tour on a spectacular loop trail through King's Palace, Papoose Room, Queen's Chamber, and Green Lake Room.

Distance: 0.75 mile
Hiking time: 1.5 hours
Difficulty: Moderately easy
Elevation gain: 80 feet; 15-step stairway to exit
Type of hike: One-way paved loop trail
Best seasons: Year-round. The underground temperature remains at 56°F.
Restrictions: Ranger-led tour by reservation only. Group size is limited to a maximum of fifty-five people. Children under four are not allowed on the tour. Anyone under age sixteen must be accompanied by an adult. No strollers, pets, or tobacco products. Stay on the trail at all times. No food or drink except bottled water. Flash photography is allowed. Not handicapped accessible.
Schedule: King's Palace Tour is daily year-round. Times and frequency of the tour varies, depending on the season. Check at the visitor center for ticket availability, dates, and times. Reservations are required for the tour. Make reservations at recreation.gov or call (877) 444-6777. Walk-in tickets may be available daily on a first-come first-served basis. Ask at the visitor center for availability. Meet at the underground lunch room and rest area 15 minutes before the start of the tour.
Maps: Park map
Trail contact: Carlsbad Caverns National Park (see appendix)

Finding the trailhead: Drive southwest from Carlsbad on US 62/180 for 20 miles to Whites City. Turn right at the signed junction on the Carlsbad Caverns Highway and drive 7 miles to the park headquarters, visitor center, and two parking lots. Buy tickets at the visitor center and take elevator down to the lunch room and rest area. The tour group meets here. Trailhead GPS: N32 10.30' / W104 26.39'

The Hike

The 0.75-mile trail on the King's Palace Tour is a spectacular ranger-led hike that leads through four decorated rooms—King's Palace, Papoose Room, Queen's Chamber, and the Green Lake Room. The route was a self-guided side trip off the Natural Entrance Trail until cave features were irreparably vandalized along the trail. The trail was turned into a ranger-guided tour in 1992 to prevent future damage.

The King's Palace Tour is by reservation and paid ticket only. To ensure that you get on a tour, especially if it's on the weekend, make a reservation at recreation.gov or call 877-444-6777. Walk-in tickets may be available on a first-come first-served basis. Ask at the ticket desk in the morning if any are available. Hiking groups are limited to a maximum of fifty-five people and children under four years old are not allowed on the tour. Children under sixteen must be accompanied by an adult.

The times and frequency of the tours vary according to the season. While tour frequency and times may change, in 2017 the National Park Service offered four daily tours from April to early September and one daily tour during the rest of the year. Hikers are advised to be at the meeting spot by the underground lunch room and restrooms 15 minutes before the scheduled trip time. Remember to wear sturdy shoes, rather than flip flops, and bring a flashlight. Either take the elevators from the visitor center or hike down the Natural Entrance Trail to the hike starting point.

The ranger leading the tour announces it shortly before the start time, and then gives a ten-minute talk about the trail, safety, and restrictions. Throughout the tour the ranger stops in each room or at important features and gives an interpretive talk. The group, led by the ranger, heads off from the lunch room down a long corridor to the junction of the Big Room and Natural Entrance trails, and heads right on the Natural Entrance Trail. It slowly climbs to the base of Iceberg Rock, where the ranger opens a gate to start the King's Palace hike.

The wide paved trail, lined with low stone walls and a metal handrail, descends 80 feet down switchbacks to the floor of a room. The trail passes cave decorations and then passes into the magnificent King's Palace. The ceiling of the large, almost circular room is crammed with glittering stalactites and hanging draperies. A 1924 National Geographic article described the ceiling: "Thousands of stalactites hang singly, in doublets, in triplets, and in groups. They range from a few inches to lengths representing the entire height of the room and in diameter from that of a small pencil to masses many feet thick." Few stalagmites grew from the room's floor since standing water inhibited their growth. Several scenes in the classic old movie *Journey to the Center of the Earth*, starring James Mason and Pat Boone, were filmed in the room in 1959.

The room, named for a castle-like formation in its center, was named along with the other rooms on this tour by young cowboy Jim White around 1901. White was the first person to seriously explore the cave, including this area, which was called the Scenic Rooms. White left charcoal smudge marks on the cave walls, some still in this area, to find his way out of the cave and marked his routes with lengths of string.

The trail squeezes through a short excavated tunnel and enters the Papoose Room, an exquisite chamber filled with slender stalactites and ribbons resembling huge bacon slices hanging from the sloped ceiling. The trail leaves the room and goes through another corridor into the Queen's Chamber, considered one of the most beautifully decorated rooms in the caverns.

The Queen's Chamber is a narrow room lined with hanging stalactites and draperies befitting an underground queen. The 42-foot-high Queen's Draperies, among the tallest in the cave, absorb light and emit it for a few seconds after a flashlight is turned off. The draperies form when masses of stalactites grow together. Sitting on the low wall along the trail, the ranger will probably tell you about the time that Jim White's kerosene lantern flickered out in this room. White, like all cavers, usually carried back-up sources of light but on that exploration of the Queen's Chamber he didn't. Stuck on the other side of the room from the lantern, White and his companion were able to find their way back to it and light the wick with three matches in his pocket. At this point the ranger turns off all the lights and the group sits in total darkness and silence for a few minutes.

The next trail section passes through a natural keyhole and enters the King's Palace opposite the entry trail. Numerous decorations including chandeliers of stalactites, standing columns, and draperies adorn the walls on this side of the palace. Look for the King's Bell Cord, a hanging, extremely thin, 7-foot-long soda straw, and a stalactite and stalagmite that are the width of a knife blade apart. Some call them the Frustrated Lovers.

The trail leaves the Palace through a short excavated tunnel and enters the Green Lake Room, a tall room lined with decorations. Past the Bashful Elephant formation, look left for a couple holes that lead to a long passageway to the

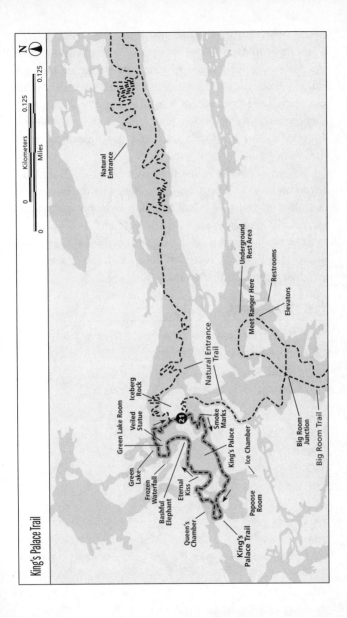

King's Palace Trail

closed New Mexico Room and a stone waterfall spilling down the cliff face. Above looms the Veiled Statue, a massive column formed when stalactite and stalagmite met and bonded about 100,000 years ago. The trail begins climbing and reaches the Green Lake, a small emerald pool tucked in a recess beside the path. The pond, filled by a steady flow of dripping water, reflects stalagmites and flowstone on the walls and ceiling above.

The trail continues climbing and then ascends a flight of fifteen metal steps. Above is a gate opened by the ranger and the end of the King's Palace Trail. Go right on the Natural Entrance Trail and retrace your step past The Boneyard back to the main junction with the Big Room Trail. Walk straight ahead at the four-way intersection to the elevators, restrooms, and underground lunch room.

Miles and Directions

0.0 Start at the closed gate on the Natural Entrance Trail.

0.4 Queen's Chamber.

0.75 Arrive back at the trailhead and Natural Entrance Trail. Go left to return to elevators and the Big Room Trail.

Appendix: Trail Contact Information

Carlsbad Caverns National Park
3225 Carlsbad Caverns Highway
Carlsbad, NM 88220
(575) 785-2232
Bat Flight Information: (575) 236-1374
www.nps.gov/cave

Guadalupe Mountains National Park
400 Pine Canyon
Salt Flat, TX 79847
Pine Springs Visitor Center: (915) 828-3251
Dog Canyon Ranger Station: (575) 981-2418
www.nps.gov/gumo

About the Author

Stewart M. Green is a veteran adventure-travel author and photographer based in Colorado Springs. Stewart has written and photographed over thirty books for FalconGuides and Globe Pequot Press, including *Rock Climbing Colorado*, *Rock Climbing Utah*, *Rock Climbing New England*, *Scenic Routes & Byways Colorado*, *Scenic Routes & Byways California's Pacific Coast*, *Best Climbs Moab*, *Best Hikes Near Colorado Springs*, and *Best Easy Day Hikes Phoenix*. He also writes and photographs for many publications, magazines, websites, and books. Stewart, a rock climber, mountaineer, hiker, and explorer, is also a Senior Climbing Guide for Front Range Climbing Company.